David

After God's Heart

Titus Chu

David: After God's Heart
by Titus Chu

First Edition: November 2005
Second Edition: April 2010
Third Edition: August 2013
PDF & Print on Demand

Distributed by
The Church in Cleveland Literature Service
3150 Warren Road
Cleveland, Ohio 44111

Available for purchase online.
Printed by CreateSpace,
an Amazon.com company.

Download the PDF version of this book at
www.MinistryMessages.org

Please send correspondence by email to
TheEditors@MinistryMessages.org

Published by
Good Land Publishers
Ann Arbor, Michigan

Contents

Preface

David was remarkable. Because he cared for what God desired, he became a blessing to God and made a real difference to God's own. He also helped others find their purpose. Together, they fought for God's need. Because of David, God accomplished what He longed after both for Himself and His people.

David established a kingdom for God. He also gained a city which God was happy to claim as His own and even allowed David to set in motion the building of His own residence there. God honored this shepherd boy; his seed became the means for God's own coming in the flesh. Jesus, in spite of all the intervening generations, was known as the Son of David. Why? Because as the Christ, He is builder of God's house, the church, which is the fulfillment of the desire of God's heart. Thus the church today has much to do with David's struggle to serve his own generation as a man after God's heart.

The chapters of this book are drawn from messages spoken by Titus Chu in July of 2005 during a young people's conference in Montreal, Canada.

May the Lord bless in these pages what matches the desire of His heart and speak to the hearts of those who read for the sake of His need in their own generation.

The editors

1

A Dark Background

One of the great names in the Bible is that of David, king of Israel. Most people know how he faced Goliath as a youth, and many appreciate the psalms he wrote. In fact, he wrote Psalm 23, the most famous psalm in the Bible. He had his faults and committed some serious sins, yet the apostle Paul tells us that David was a man after God's own heart (Acts 13:22) and a man who served his own generation (Acts 13:36). Even though he did some terrible things for which he paid a great price, David was still able to serve his generation in a manner that was after God's own heart.

Serving Our Generation according to God's Heart

These are the two things we should care about above everything else—our relationship with God and how we serve our generation. We should serve our generation according to God's heart. We should not merely care for our own things. Too many people either serve only themselves or serve their generation in a way that is not according to God's heart. Most people seek what is to their own benefit. Shouldn't we consider our livelihood? Yes, we should. Yet David gave himself to live for what God desired and trusted that God was able to take care of him. Today God is still looking for those who care about what He is seeking. As we serve our generation, God is looking to see if we care for what is on His heart. These two matters should regulate our lives.

As we become involved with activities, these often take on the preeminence which rightfully belongs to the Lord. The things we might feel are serving our generation for Christ, such as preaching the gospel, leading Bible studies, and so on, can merely be Christian things for us to do. These same activities can also be the means for us to care for what is really in the Lord's heart. If we preach the gospel and yet remain fruitless, we should ask why. The Bible tells us that if we fail to abide in Christ—if we fail to care for what is on His heart—we "cannot bear fruit" (John 15:4).

There are thousands of believers who love the Lord and are doing many things in His name, yet how many really care for God's heart? Some young people's events today involve contemporary music. When older Christians voice concern about this, the young people defend what has been helpful to them. The issue, however, is not what kind of music we are using but doing what pleases the Lord. Regardless how things may appear outwardly, our criteria must be that the Lord Himself is satisfied and His need is met.

Serving the Lord, Not Ourselves

I know some Christians who faithfully preach the gospel, then hold onto their converts as an asset. They display these converts in the meetings as living proof of their own Christian fruitfulness, forcing them to stand up and say something. Though such Christians are faithful to preach the gospel, they have no idea what God's heart's desire is, and those they bring to Christ are often not able to grow well.

Our Bible knowledge can be profitable to God, but it can also become our own personal Christian asset. If we use what we know for our own gain, we are not truly after God's heart. I do not mean that we should not give ourselves to learn and be equipped. We should use every opportunity to study the Word and minister to others the light we receive. We should also lead people to Christ, shepherd them, and serve in our church. We should all be aggressive to learn these things. Every one of us must seek to become as profitable to the Lord as possible. If we are people after God's heart, we will seek to use what the Lord has given us for His profit.

Focusing on God's Heart

There is a great difference between being according to God's heart and doing things for God. Doing things for God with no realization of God's heart has little meaning. We should focus on what God is after. As we confront the practical realities of life, such as career and family, what is our focus? Too often, it is not the Lord. Even in our Christian service, we may do things without touching God's heart. If we realize the importance of knowing God's heart, our service will be healthy, and we will be blessed.

We all need to consider why we do what we do. For instance, if you are a student, why did you choose the college you attend? You may respond, "I want to have a good career." Why? "So I can get married and raise a family." Again, why? So you can have grandchildren? What is your goal?

Even in smaller matters we should ask ourselves this question. Suppose you like to buy spiritual books. Ask yourself why. You may answer, "I am trying to acquire a good library." Why? Perhaps you would eventually admit, "I want to be respected as a spiritual brother." Dare we ask why one more time? Many faithful, zealous Christians live out their entire lives without ever answering the question, "Why am I doing this?" The Lord today is hard-pressed to find anyone who cares about what is on His heart. We may live our lives piously, admirably, and even faithfully, but unless our goal is the Lord's profit, He will not find His satisfaction in us.

A proper relationship with God involves our person. The right kind of person is one according to God's heart. Once our person is right before God, we can properly serve our generation. This sounds simple, but it is difficult to live out.

Beloved in Spite of Failure

Paul, Peter, John, Stephen, and even the Lord Jesus all spoke of David. How could a flawed man who committed such great sins become so appreciated? How could he be held up as someone who was according to God's heart and who served his generation? In many ways Saul, the first king of Israel, seemed a better man. God, however, rejected Saul and cherished David. Even the meaning of David's name is "beloved" (Brown). Yet how could God love him when he failed so seriously?

As we read about David, we should be encouraged. May we each tell the Lord, "You know how I fail and how unworthy I feel I am, Lord, yet I still want to be according to Your heart and serve my generation as a proper person." Without this, many leaders may damage those they lead and do or say things that cause real problems. When it comes to serving the Lord, none are qualified. Therefore, we should be encouraged that the Lord could appreciate someone like David, who, because his heart was right, could still be so greatly used by the Lord. The Lord considered David to be one of His greatest servants. Because of this, I hope we each would tell the Lord, "I give myself to be a person after Your heart, Lord, no matter how discouraging things may be. I may fail and suffer defeat at times. I may even get caught in something very ugly, yet I still want to be a person after Your heart and serve my generation for You."

Priests, Kings, and Prophets

In order to understand the phrase "who served his own generation" (Acts 13:36), we have to consider what the situation of David's generation was.

God worked through three types of people in the Old Testament. Initially, He worked through the priesthood. The priests brought the people before God and brought God's word to the people. God desired to maintain His testimony with His people through the priesthood. Many times, however, the priests failed, so the Lord raised up a second group made up of judges, and then kings, to rule over His people.

There were times, however, when neither the priesthood nor the kingship functioned properly. During those times, the Lord raised up a third group, the prophets. The priests brought God's people to Himself, the kings brought His rule to the people, and the prophets spoke for God directly. Through these three types of servants—priests, kings, and prophets—God operated among His people. When all three were functioning as intended, as they did during the reign of David, the situation among God's people was healthy, and God had His testimony among His people.

Requirements for a Healthy Local Church

Today, if the local church or group of believers we fellowship with is to be healthy, it needs to have people who function in these three capacities—as priests, kings, and prophets.

First, we need some who are living before the Lord as today's priests. By living and praying in Christ's presence, they are able to bring others into His presence also. This is what is represented by the priesthood. Genuine priests are those who are able to bring man to God and God to man. A local church that is lacking people who are exercised in this way will be weak.

Second, there is a need for healthy leadership. There must be some who are able to execute what God desires so that the believers can go forward. This is what is represented by the kingship. The genuine kingship carries forward what God desires. Without proper leadership, a local church will be messy—there will be no clear direction about what should be done, and this may lead to disagreement among the members.

Third, the Lord's speaking must be present through those who are able to function as prophets, for apart from the Lord's divine speaking, His people cannot know Him as the living God among them. A church that lacks some who function as prophets will experience deadness in their gatherings.

I am afraid, however, that very few among us live as priests before God. Only a few gather to pray at the designated times of prayer or have a time of personal prayer. Therefore, most flunk the first matter necessary for a healthy church life. Furthermore, few are willing to shepherd others. Therefore, most also flunk the second requirement, that of being shepherds and leaders. Finally, I am afraid that most also fail to speak for the Lord. Yet if any local church is short in any of these three categories, the Lord will not be able to operate to the extent He desires.

Israel under the Judges

Due to the degradation among the priests after the Israelites entered into the promised land, God raised up judges to rule His people. The first three judges—Othniel, Ehud, and Shamgar—must have ruled well, for the Bible records very little about them (Judg. 3). When we come to Gideon, however, the peculiar stories begin. Gideon began well. He responded to the Lord's call and led his small band of Israelites against the immense army of Midian as the Lord commanded. He gained a great victory for Israel. After this, however, he made a golden ephod and set it up in his city. All Israel came to worship it, playing the harlot after an idol (Judg. 6–8).

The most famous of the judges is Samson (Judg. 13–16). Everyone admires him for his single-handed victories over the Philistines, but eventually he was tricked by a woman and fell captive to the Philistines. In his final victory, he pulled down their temple so that "the dead that he killed at his death were more than he had killed in his life" (Judg. 16:30). When we read his final prayer, however, we realize that his heart was not set on God's interest but on personal revenge. He should have confessed what a poor judge he had been and asked the Lord to raise up someone who could do better.

None of the judges seemed to exhibit any interest in what was really on God's heart. They were raised up to judge God's people, but none of them asked God how they should judge or what would truly please Him. They should have asked Him, "How should I be with Your people? How can I represent You if I do not know what is in Your heart? Reveal Your heart to me."

Serving according to God's Heart

An obedient son does what he thinks his parents want. If his parents tell him to study, he studies diligently. His grades reflect his hard work. Being a good student, however, does not make this son a person after his father's heart. Are high marks what his father is really after? Being obedient to his parents and being a person after his parents' heart may be two different things. It was the same with the judges and God. They were surely trying to serve God the best they could, but not one served God as a person after His heart.

Christians get involved with many good spiritual things. Some even give their lives to serve God and become very busy. You cannot say that God is not happy with them, just as you cannot say that a parent is not happy with an obedient child. However, we must ask ourselves: Are the spiritual things we do really according to God's heart? What we do may seem so right, yet it may not be according to His heart at all. Oh, how we need to see this! Paul tells us that in David God found someone who was after His own heart. He had found someone who could really serve Him in his generation. Some who led God's people prior to David did a competent job but never knew what God was after. We can act according to God's laws and principles, but if we are not after His heart, He will not be happy with us, regardless how successful or victorious we are. The Lord desires someone who cares about what He cares about. What God values is not how capable we are but whether or not we care for what is in His heart.

Once we discover what is on the Lord's heart, we should give our lives to fight for it. David was such a fighter. Too many today are distracted from what the Lord has revealed to them of His purpose. We need to be saved from doing spiritual things with only those things in view. Too often we consider how things will affect or bless others. Instead, we should consider how those things affect or bless the Lord.

We may consider how to please our parents, spouse, or others. There may be many people we try to please more than the Lord. Actually, the person we want to please the most is ourselves. It seems we have many bosses. Even in spiritual matters, we may consider what we do in light of others, not the Lord. A spiritual person, however, considers what is profitable to the Lord, trusting other people to Him.

None of the judges thought to seek what was really in God's heart. We also may be very busy doing things in the Lord's name, but are we charged by seeing what is in His heart? God is not after project leaders; He is after those who seek Him and serve according to His heart.

The Failure of the Priests, Judges, and Prophets

The judges carried out their commitment before the Lord, but among them God did not find anyone who was after His own heart. Eventually, the priests failed, the judges failed, and even the prophets failed. That was the situation leading up to David's generation. Eli, the last judge prior to Samuel, was also a priest, yet in some ways he seemed to be as blind spiritually as he became physically. Concerning this time, the Bible says, "The word of the Lord was rare in those days; there was no widespread revelation" (1 Sam. 3:1). Still, we are told that the lamp of the Lord had not yet gone out (1 Sam. 3:3). Praise the Lord for this! The situation was not totally hopeless, yet there was little, if any, of God's speaking among the people.

The Degradation of Israel

So what was the condition of Israel in the time of the judges? Due to the shortage among the priests, the judges, and the prophets, the condition of the people degenerated. With all three of these groups becoming dysfunctional, the situation among God's people went from bad to worse. Not only did the people fall into confusion and immorality, but they even began slaughtering one another within the land (Judg. 20).

Beginning with Judges 17, a series of events occurred which illustrate how poor the situation had become. A man named Micah stole some money from his mother but then returned it to her. Having dedicated the money to the Lord, she had some of it made into two images. These were set up for worship in Micah's house. He even made an ephod (a garment for a priest), first setting up one of his own sons, and then a Levite, to act as priest! Men from the tribe of Dan then came along, stole his idols, and carried off his priest to the north country, where they established their own shrine.

After this, a Levite's concubine was abused and killed by a group of Benjaminites, whereupon the Levite cut her into twelve pieces and sent the pieces throughout all Israel (Judg. 19). All the people gathered together as one man in Mizpah to learn what had happened. When they heard what the men of Benjamin had done, the tribes of Israel went to war with the entire tribe of Benjamin, for the leaders of Benjamin would not surrender the guilty men for judgment. At first Benjamin defeated the rest of Israel, killing twenty-two thousand Israelites the first day, then eighteen thousand the next. Eventually, however, the people of Israel asked the Lord if they should continue to fight, and the Lord responded that He would deliver Benjamin into their hands in the next battle. The Israelites did defeat Benjamin, killing twenty-five thousand soldiers. They went on to burn their cities, killing all the inhabitants. Only six hundred men managed to escape. All the tribes had suffered in this calamity, but what happened to Benjamin was by far the most disastrous, for the entire tribe had been nearly wiped from the face of the earth (Judg. 20).

Afterwards the children of Israel sought a way to restore Benjamin, for the six hundred remaining Benjaminite men had no wives, and the other tribes had vowed not to give their daughters to marry a Benjaminite. Eventually they came up with a solution: One city had not obeyed the summons to go to war against Benjamin, so they killed all the inhabitants of that city, sparing only four hundred virgin girls, whom they gave to the men of Benjamin. They told the remaining two hundred men to hide in the vineyards during the annual feast at Shiloh and steal wives for themselves from among the daughters of Israel who came to dance. In this way, if their daughters were taken, technically they would not be breaking their vow (Judg. 21).

All these stories provide a good picture of how confused the situation was among God's people at that time when it came to the worship of God! Where was the priesthood? How could a Levite function as a priest? How could Jehovah be worshiped with idols? We see how violent and immoral the people had become through the account of the Levite and his concubine. It is unbelievable that one tribe could even pray to God about going up against another tribe in battle. God may have given them permission, but was asking such a thing according to His heart? Was God happy with such intercession? Did He feel, "Yes, hallelujah, tomorrow you may slaughter each other some more"? This did not glorify God. Yet how often Christians approach God with prayers like this rather than with prayers that are after His heart!

God's Permission versus God's Heart

God's leading and God's heart can be two different things. God's word in answer to Israel's prayer may have given them the false assurance they were doing His will, just as we might feel when we finally receive an answer to something we have prayed for. Afterward we might say, "I am only doing what God told me to do!" Yet when we prayed, were we asking according to His heart? You may tell others that the Lord has led you in a certain matter, but those with spiritual understanding will realize that, although the Lord indeed may have given you permission, it was not something according to His heart.

Not one person on the whole earth at that time seemed to care about what God wanted. No one was focused upon God's heart. Israel's commitment to honor their own vow not to allow their daughters to marry the sons of Benjamin seemed to be more important than God Himself. Surely they did not know God's heart. They just did whatever they felt bound to do. The book of Judges ends, "In those days there was no king in Israel; everyone did what was right in his own eyes" (Judg. 21:25). What kind of people were these that God called His own?

Why would God call such a group of senseless people? Yet even in the midst of this era of the judges, God still kept a few, such as Ruth and Boaz, the great-grandparents of David, who shined before Him. May the Lord cause us to realize how much we need to be freed from all religious concepts and practices so we may simply and purely care for the Lord's heart. Everything around us may be dark and seemingly hopeless, but if we remain pure toward God and inquire of Him what He desires, God can yet have a way to gain what He is after.

David: A Man after God's Heart

This is the environment that led to David. How precious that on the earth, even in the midst of such darkness and confusion and in spite of his own flaws and weaknesses, David realized God desired something and sought out His heart. Because of this one man, an entire generation was brought into God's blessing.

2 | God's Preparation— A Woman, Her Son, and a King

During the time of the judges, the situation among the children of Israel had fallen very low. The priests had failed, the judges had failed, and there seemed to be no prophet the Lord could send to speak for Him. During this dark period, the Lord's testimony among His people was very weak. The tribe of Benjamin was nearly annihilated by the other tribes. God allowed this confused situation to continue for a long time. After about four hundred fifty years (Acts 13:20), however, God was ready to change the age.

Hannah's Vow

In order to change the age, God required a woman who was pure enough to offer Him her own child. This woman was Hannah (1 Sam. 1:2). In most regards, Hannah did not stand out from others. Her name means "favored" (Strong) or "gracious" (Hitchcock), which all females generally are. Her husband had a second wife who bore him children, yet Hannah remained barren. This, however, did not affect his love or affection for her (v. 5).

Hannah could not accept this barrenness and traveled all the way to the Lord's dwelling in Shiloh to beseech the Lord for a son. In her prayer, she vowed to the Lord that, should He give her a son, she would offer him back to the Lord to serve Him all his life, and that no razor would come upon his head (v. 11). In other words, she would offer her son as a Nazarite (Num. 6:1–5), someone who would be qualified to serve before the Lord even though he was not born a priest. In effect, Hannah was saying, "I don't want a son for myself; I want a son for You."

Hannah and Eli

Hannah was praying so desperately that Eli accused her of being drunk (1 Sam. 1:12–14). Eli was both the high priest and judge of Israel, so for him to rebuke Hannah like this was not a small thing. As we are purely seeking the Lord for His interest, sometimes He will allow us to be misjudged and rebuked by His servants. This is hard to take, but we must appreciate how Hannah responded. She did not indignantly say, "Can't you see that I am praying? I am not drunk! Apologize!" Even to one so quick to misjudge, she responded with a proper attitude. She did not seek to vindicate herself. Instead, she told Eli that she was bitter of soul due to the heaviness in her heart. Eli then immediately realized the real nature of the situation and spoke a word representing the Lord, indicating that he did indeed possess spiritual insight.

How do we know that Hannah received Eli's word as being from the Lord? She immediately went and ate and was encouraged. She had the assurance that the Lord had heard her prayer. This indicates again something impressive about her. How could she believe the word of a person who had just demonstrated his lack of discernment? Hadn't Eli just misjudged her for being a drunkard? How is it that she could then trust Eli's word that the Lord would answer her prayer? Hannah recognized Eli was still the Lord's representative, regardless of his personal failures and flaws.

Hannah is a good model for us. Though Eli had faded as a spiritual man, he was still judge and high priest. He was able to speak for the Lord with clarity even after he was exposed as being wrong in his judgment. Even though he didn't know what Hannah had prayed, he encouraged her, assuring her that the Lord would answer her prayer.

One day, when I was a young believer, I was sorrowful before the Lord concerning a matter that weighed heavily upon my heart. A church elder saw me and rebuked me, and as I cried, he rebuked me again and commanded me to stop weeping. I did, and by the Lord's mercy I honored him as someone whom the Lord had placed over me for my care. At that moment, I realized how grave the situation was. To my feeling, if I reacted improperly I would have lost my unclouded relationship with Christ and His church, for to my feeling that elder represented both.

Hannah's Response

Thus let us all learn something more in Hannah's word. Her response to the one who had misjudged her was, "Let your maidservant find favor in your sight" (1 Sam. 1:18). If we learn to respond in this way whenever someone is critical of us, we could be saved from so many problems in the church life! Just be prepared. In the church life, there are many opportunities to be misunderstood. Even if others charge that what you are doing is terrible, learn to say, "May I find favor in your sight." This is the secret of having a healthy church life. Often the more we try to defend something, the more we open the door to further accusation. It is not a small thing to be able to respond as Hannah did. If we are able to respond so sweetly, it will open the door to a sweet church life where everyone is for the Lord and loves Him. Others don't have the intention of doing anything damaging. They just see things differently. In the church life, let us all find favor in one another's sight.

Samuel the Nazarite

Immediately after this, Hannah realized God had heard her and answered her prayer. She allowed herself to be encouraged, and indeed she did bear a son and named him Samuel, meaning "asked of God" or "heard of God" (Hitchcock).

When Samuel was young, serving in God's house, he wore the linen ephod, which means he served as a priest. He was not a Levite, but because he was offered as a Nazarite, he was separated unto the Lord and could fill in as a priest before God.

How we dress ourselves spiritually before the Lord is very important, for this determines how we serve. Even when we dress casually on the outside, inwardly we should be girded up, wearing the linen ephod, serving as priests. The day we put on the linen ephod is the day we begin to serve as priests. It is not something to be put on and taken off as we please. If we do, it means that instead of living and serving as priests, we are only participating in certain things in the church life.

Serving the Lord under Eli

Samuel served the Lord as a priest, which was made more difficult because he had to serve under Eli, whose eyes had begun to grow dim (1 Sam. 3:1–2). To serve under anyone who is not too clear can be a real dealing. If those taking the lead in a church are not clear, many drastic things can happen. Serious problems that should be handled may not be dealt with, and positive things, such as the move of the Spirit, may be missed. If we, like Samuel, have the right kind of heart, we can learn from both the negative and positive in others.

Many years ago, I discovered that a church elder smoked cigarettes. I didn't mention this to anyone, but one day a companion of mine told me he had seen this elder smoking and didn't know what to do. We could have criticized this elder or spread gossip about him, but instead I said, "Let's pray." That was a salvation. We did not pray about this elder's situation in particular, because even that could have been judgmental, opening the door to a loss of respect for him. Instead, we prayed that the Lord would have mercy upon us, so that we would only see Christ in the church life. Not long afterward, that elder gave a message in which he said, "You do not even know the power a little three-inch cigarette can have over you."

I sensed that he had had a breakthrough in this matter, and I praised the Lord. I believe our prayer played a real part in this, even though in our prayer we never directly mentioned his habit.

Those who are young in the Lord may believe the church leaders must be overcoming giants of the faith, when in fact they are just as human as everybody else. The church life is full of people who all have problems. For every problem you see in the church life, there are many more you do not see. Be thankful that you don't! In fact, if you want to be a person who is after God's heart, you must learn not to see certain things, or at least to cover them in love (1 Pet. 4:8). If you know how to handle the messiness in the church life, you will grow. In fact, the messy situations are especially for our learning and growth.

Samuel was thus serving as a priest—not on his own, but rather under a high priest whose eyesight was no longer clear. It was under these conditions, however, that the Lord spoke to him.

God's Judgment on Eli

The word of the Lord was rare in those days (1 Sam. 3:1). Israel had not heard God's voice for quite some time. Remember, the prophets had failed, along with the priests and the judges. Then one night, as Samuel was asleep in the house of the Lord, he was awakened by someone calling his name (v. 4). Samuel, never having heard the Lord's voice before, thought it must be Eli, so he ran to him. Eli told him he was mistaken and to go back to sleep. This was repeated twice more, after which Eli finally realized it was the Lord Himself who was speaking to Samuel.

Eli was clear when he needed to be clear. Though he mistook Hannah for being drunk, when he blessed her, it was a real blessing. In the same way, once he realized that the Lord was calling Samuel, he was very clear about what Samuel should do. He told Samuel to go back and when he heard the speaking again, to reply, "Speak, Lord, for Your servant hears" (v. 9). Eli might have wondered why the Lord was talking to Samuel instead of himself, for wasn't he Israel's judge and God's anointed priest? The Lord's speaking to Samuel rather than Eli already signaled God's judgment upon Eli.

When the Lord called to Samuel the fourth time, Samuel responded as Eli had told him, and the Lord spoke to Samuel of His judgment upon Eli's house. This was a very severe word. God was angry with Eli for not keeping his two sons from evil, which involved both gross immorality in God's own sanctuary and the abuse of their priestly privilege. God did not temper His judgment upon Eli just because he had faithfully raised up Samuel. It was a judgment that God said would cause tingling in the ears of all those who heard of it in Israel (1 Sam. 3:11).

Eli must have known that the word of the Lord to Samuel had something to do with him. Samuel did not want to tell Eli all that God had spoken, for God told him that Eli's house was judged with no possibility of repentance. Eli must have realized all this, for he told Samuel to hold nothing back. And, when he heard the Lord's word, he said, "It is the Lord. Let Him do what seems good to Him" (3:18). Although he did not control his sons and his eyesight had grown dim, Eli was still a spiritual man.

Samuel as Prophet, Priest, and Judge

From this point on, the Lord was manifestly with Samuel. He was recognized as a prophet in Israel (1 Sam. 3:20) and soon began to act as judge and priest (7:6, 9, 15). In Samuel we see a recovery of all three lines in one person—prophet, priest, and judge. Throughout Samuel's life, God continued to speak to him, and he did not allow even one of his words to "fall to the ground" (3:19).

God used Hannah and Samuel, the boy she offered, to draw closer to His goal. Now He needed one more person to bring in the man who would be after His heart.

Saul

Saul was the third person God needed to usher in David. His name means "desired" (Brown), "asked" (Strong), or "lent" (Hitchcock). It may also mean "ditch" (Hitchcock). Samuel's name means "asked of God," but Saul's name merely means "asked." Saul was man's desire, asked for by man. When the people asked Samuel for a king (1 Sam. 8:5), Saul was God's answer to their request. In a sense, Saul was like a ditch that had to be crossed over before David could come forth, but we shouldn't look down on such ditches, for without them, life would be very flat. Saul may have been a frustration, but his life also provides a colorful backdrop to the process that brought forth David, enhancing our appreciation of what God would eventually gain in him.

Israel Wanting a King

The people approached Samuel to choose a king for them. It is hard to fault them when we consider the children of Israel's experience under the judges. The situation was often chaotic. At times they were without a judge; no one was in charge. Whenever the need arose, however, God would raise someone up. So judges ruled only sporadically over the four hundred plus years they were in the good land. Even when they did rule, the situation was often very peculiar. Therefore, the people asked Samuel for a king to rule over them as they saw in the nations around them.

God didn't want to give them a king because He wanted them to rely upon Him. Even when God gave them a judge, He did not allow them to feel overly secure, for when people feel safe and secure, they tend to forget about Him. Like the people of Israel, we often desire a "king" just as the godless people around us do. But God's desire is that we would depend upon Him. When we have money in the bank, a roof over our heads, and food on the table, do we feel the need to cling to God? It is when we have problems we pray more.

When Samuel brought this matter to the Lord, the Lord told him, "Heed the voice of the people in all that they say to you; for they have not rejected you, but they have rejected Me, that I should not reign over them" (1 Sam. 8:7). The Lord wanted to be Israel's king, but when they refused Him, He gave them another as king. In doing so, however, He intended that He would be the king over that king. This required a man after His own heart.

Samuel Anointing Saul King

The man chosen from among the Israelites to be their king was Saul, a good man of a choice family. "There was not a more handsome person than he among the children of Israel. From his shoulders upward he was taller than any of the people" (1 Sam. 9:2). He must have appeared to be the right choice.

Samuel anointed Saul king. He "took a flask of oil and poured it on his head, and kissed him and said: Is it not because the Lord has anointed you commander over His inheritance?" (10:1). Samuel did not make such a speech when he anointed David. I believe Samuel really liked Saul. Thus Saul was anointed to be the first king over God's inheritance, the nation of Israel. And as Saul, the new king, turned to leave and go forth, God gave him a new heart (v. 9). What a confirmation! He became another person, no longer fearful. Then the Spirit of the Lord came upon him so that he spoke among the prophets (v. 10).

I hope many would desire what Saul experienced at this time. We should not be satisfied to remain the same. We should ask God to anoint us until we become a different person, someone filled with the Holy Spirit. When others see us, they should feel they are seeing a new person. O how we need a new heart that comes from being filled with the Spirit! Our church life should not be in a set, predictable pattern. It should be filled with people saturated with the Spirit. God is moving, and we are moving with Him! He is buoyant and vital, and we must be the same. Lord, fill us with Your Spirit! O Lord, saturate us! Make us new!

3

Saul—
The Insufficiency
of Religion

For the past three thousand years, Saul has been held up as the "bad king" next to David, the "good king." Those who think of Saul as being bad, however, should read the biblical account, for Saul was actually rather good. Yes, he tried to hunt down and kill David, but when he was anointed, he had a very good start: he was given a new heart, the Spirit came upon him, and he valiantly fought against the enemies of Israel. He was not a terrible person, but he had a sad end. How was it that he failed to satisfy God's heart?

Saul's Humble Start

Saul was not initially yearning after power. Though he wanted no part in being king, it was thrust upon him. When Samuel told Saul he would be king, Saul responded very humbly, saying that he was not worthy of such an honor. He probably knew that being king would cause a lot of headaches, so he wasn't interested. Samuel, however, anointed him king anyway, and the Lord gave him a new heart (1 Sam. 10:9).

A little while later, when the king was to be publicly chosen by lot from among God's people, it seems Saul was still hoping it would not be him. After all, the chances of being chosen by lot from among so many people seemed remote. But once the tribe of Benjamin was chosen, and then his clan was chosen from among Benjamin, Saul probably began to realize Samuel might have been right. Thus, by the time his name was called, Saul was nowhere to be found. The people had to ask God where he was, and God had to tell them he was hiding among all the baggage (10:22). No one could have accused Saul of being ambitious for the kingship!

Saul was probably grateful for having been given a new heart and being filled with the Spirit (10:9–10). He might have said, "Thank you for everything, it's a great honor...but I think there's been some mistake. I don't want to be king!" Yet when the people looked at him after finding him among the piles of tents and luggage, they saw that he was indeed attractive and stood head and shoulders above the rest. No one else seemed as qualified as him.

Saul Established as King of Israel

At this point, the Ammonites invaded Israel and encamped against Jabesh Gilead, a city of Israel (1 Sam. 11:1). The people of that city asked to be given seven days to seek a deliverer in Israel, and the enemy surprisingly agreed to this. If no one could be found to defeat the Ammonites, however, the people were to surrender, their right eyes were to be plucked out, and they were to serve the Ammonites as slaves. If they did not surrender, the entire population would be put to the sword.

When Saul heard of the situation, the Spirit of God came upon him, and he slew a yoke of oxen and sent the pieces throughout Israel, saying the oxen of whoever did not respond to his summons would suffer the same fate (11:6–7). As a result, 300,000 men assembled before him at Mizpah, with 30,000 of Judah, and they totally defeated the Ammonites and freed Jabesh Gilead. Immediately afterward, Saul was established as the true leader in the eyes of the people and publicly received as king by all Israel in Gilgal.

Before this battle, some worthless rebels had despised Saul and questioned his ability to save Israel from its enemies, but Saul had held his peace (10:27). Now that Saul had won this great victory, the people said to Samuel, "Who is he who said, 'Shall Saul reign over us?' Bring the men, that we may put them to death." Saul, however, said that no one would be put to death and that it was the Lord who accomplished salvation in Israel (11:12–13). Saul's kingship was off to a good start. He had potential for becoming a great king. If Saul had been allowed to die at this point, he would have been remembered as a very promising young king.

Israel had been in a desperate situation, with the Philistines occupying the northwest coast while the Ammonites threatened from the east. In Saul, the people thought they had found the right man to face this difficult situation. However, they were not accustomed to having a king. They had no idea what they were getting into. They had no way of knowing what having such a king would be like until they experienced it. They lived in sensations rather than reality, and the heady notion of having a king led them into making Saul king. As time went on, they found that having a king was not as they dreamed it would be. To this God could say, "I tried to warn you, but you insisted."

Religion Defined

It was God who made Saul king over His people. To rule as king was Saul's divine commitment. Yet, as the remaining years of his rule demonstrate, he did not satisfy God's heart. As the divinely-appointed king, Saul had to handle many situations, but he did so by means of God's rival—the self-life.

After Saul was made king, he felt responsible to take care of God's people. The kingdom he ruled over, however, was actually God's, not his own. God's intention was that He would exercise His kingship through Saul, who would represent Him before the people. Instead, however, Saul tried to take care of whatever was needed on his own without God, the true King.

The needs of God's people are real, and they must be taken care of. Is that reason enough to act? No, it isn't, because God Himself desires to be the One who meets His people's needs.

Therefore, we should not respond to a need apart from God, for when we do, we fall into religion. Due to his religious response, Saul lost his value before God as a man who could rule for Him. Rather than responding to needs directly, as Saul did, let us go to the Lord to seek His heart.

When we are honored by God with some responsibility as Saul was, our immediate response is usually to try to be faithful to what has been committed to us. This often takes the form of doing what is right, what is necessary, or what is expected. When we do things for God in this way, however, we are being religious, because we do them apart from God. Even this book could cause you to do something that will only be religious if it is not of God Himself. Whenever we think, "That's it!" or "This is the way!" then we should realize we need to stop ourselves and check with the Lord. All such things can lead us into religion if they become a means for us to do something for God independent of Him in our self-life.

Saul was very good in so many ways, yet he failed to satisfy God, not because he was evil but because he was religious. His religious nature offended the Lord.

Offering without Seeking God

Israel was threatened by an immense army of Philistines, "as the sand which is on the seashore" (1 Sam. 13:5). Before going into battle against this army, Saul wanted Samuel to offer a burnt offering and peace offering on Israel's behalf. Samuel, however, had not yet arrived. Saul waited for him not simply for a day or two, but seven days, according to the time Samuel appointed. Many among Israel had already gone into hiding, and the people with Saul in Gilgal were beginning to desert him. Saul, as king, felt he must act. Not wanting to go into battle without first sacrificing to the Lord, he proceeded to offer the burnt offering without Samuel. Just as he finished, however, Samuel arrived.

If the Bible did not record that Samuel later mourned for Saul (16:1), it would be tempting to believe Samuel's timing was intentional. Samuel gave no apology, nor did he explain why he had been late. He simply said, "You have done foolishly. You have not kept the commandment of the Lord your God, which He commanded you. For now the Lord would have established your kingdom over Israel forever. But now your kingdom shall not continue. The Lord has sought for Himself *a man after His own heart*, and the Lord has commanded him to be commander over His people, because you have not kept what the Lord commanded you" (13:13–14).

Saul must have been crushed by this word. It seems he would have been justified to say he had never sought to be king in the first place. Anyway, wasn't God's giving irrevocable (Rom. 11:29)? And since Samuel and God had forced the kingship upon him, should not Samuel have at least stayed with him rather than leaving him to try to take care of things by himself? And wasn't the whole reason he was forced to offer the sacrifice because Samuel was tardy? Wasn't then Samuel the one who was responsible for all his hardship?

It is hard not to sympathize with Saul in this situation. It is not easy to see what he had done wrong. God had given him the kingship, a responsibility that Saul did not even want, but one he was trying to faithfully carry out. As he waited for Samuel, the enemy gained strength while his own numbers dwindled. Didn't God expect him to save Israel?

Saul should have asked God Himself what to do. If he had, God might have told him to offer the sacrifice. Samuel then would have had nothing to say. But Saul's feeling was, "It's all on my shoulders. I must do the job I have been chosen to do." He sought to handle the situation as the circumstances dictated rather than seek God's direction.

This story should cause us to wonder what the Lord wants from us. As believers, we should never declare, "I must do it" or "I have no choice." Instead, we should always seek the Lord until we are able to say, "The Lord told me."

The main thing we must see is that Saul did not involve God at all in his decision. Therefore, Saul acted religiously. God wanted to lead Saul in his decisions, to be with him as he carried them out, and to be present in the results. Instead, Saul just did what he thought he was supposed to do. This is religion: doing everything we think God wants us to do, yet God Himself not being involved.

God's Heart versus Religion

The biggest enemy we face as believers is not sin or the world but religion. Religion is the biggest frustration to our individual growth in following the Lord, and it is the biggest frustration to the building up of the body of Christ, the church. Instead of living a religious life, let us live by Christ and take Him in everything.

God's heart is that we would do everything with Him, in Him, and according to Him. This is the way He wants us to do everything that we do for Him. Because Saul was not seeking the Lord in this way, he could not rule as God's king over His people. This may seem severe, but Saul was not a person after God's heart; he was just a good religious man doing what he thought a good king should do. His actions did not originate with the Lord. To God, however, this is what counts. Had Saul carried out his kingship by casting himself upon God, God would have established his kingdom (1 Sam. 13:13). Saul, however, was not a man after God's heart; he was just a good man trying to do the right thing.

What satisfies God? Christ. When we have Christ, experience Him, and minister to Him, God is satisfied. Yet how many Christians today—and even churches—feel they must do this or that because it is the right thing to do, rather than because the Lord led them to do it?

Not Utterly Destroying Amalek

Soon afterward, Saul again displayed this fundamental problem. God wanted the Amalekites utterly destroyed (1 Sam. 15:3), yet Saul kept alive the king and the best of the livestock (v. 9). He may have thought that such good livestock shouldn't be wasted, but rather used as offerings for his previous failures.

When Saul attacked the Amalekites, he probably intended to carry out God's command to utterly destroy them from the face of the earth, but once he saw how fine their sheep and goats were, he relented and preserved alive what he deemed best, thinking it would please Samuel to have such for offerings (v. 15).

Any idol that a believer possesses should be destroyed. What if, however, that idol is of great value? Some idols are treasured as artwork and are highly valued by collectors. Wouldn't it be reasonable, if an idol was valued at many thousands of dollars, to sell it to a collector, and then donate the money to the work of the Lord? We may easily destroy a cheap idol, but what of an idol that is of great value? I hope you would destroy it! God does not need such offerings. He is able to provide whatever His people need.

Jealously Protecting His Throne

As we'll see later, Saul made David his personal musician, and eventually, the leader of his armies. David became known as a great warrior, and the women began to sing about his many victories (1 Sam. 18:7). The long rows of colorfully-dressed women dancing, playing tambourines, and singing in this way must have really been something to watch. But their boasting in David caused Saul to feel his throne was being threatened. Therefore, as David played his harp to soothe him, Saul threw his spear at him, thinking to kill him by pinning him to the wall! He actually tried this twice (v. 11). He knew the Lord was with David, yet he sought to kill him to protect his throne. His jealousy was prompted by the women's admiration and promotion of David above himself.

Saul probably felt justified to seek David's life, for if David was anointed, Saul would have to die before David could take the throne. It may have seemed to Saul that God was using

David to bring about his death. So, to Saul, it was David or him. Saul's argument with God could have been, "I did not choose to be anointed king. You arranged the casting of the lot, and You even told the people where I was hiding and had me brought out. And now You want to terminate me? Aren't Your gifts irrevocable?" Saul certainly had a right to honor his own kingship since it was given to him by the Lord, but he should not have tried to kill David. He should have simply tried to carry out his kingship in a way that furthered the Lord's interests. The Lord, however, was unable to use Saul as a king who would rule His people according to His heart.

Many people who gain a position of influence try to hold on to it, even if it means sacrificing others to do it. Even in the realm of Christian work, we can see how some at times have been willing to sacrifice others in order to protect what they feel is their place. As we serve the Lord, it is easy to feel that things would be much better if certain people were not there. If they are finally driven out or moved aside, we are peaceful about it, thinking it will now be easier for us to go on. If something has truly been given to us by the Lord, however, we do not have to worry about someone taking it away from us. Instead, we should care for the profit of those who are with us and trust the Lord to carry out what He wants to do, for it is His work, not ours.

Watchman Nee wrote a hymn saying that when others stretched out their hands against him and began to struggle with one another, he shut his door and sang hymns to the Lord. He realized that it was the Lord who suffered the most. The Lord takes no joy when Christians fight among themselves over who should submit to whom, and what will happen if they do not.

Presuming to Choose His Successor

In 1 Samuel 20:31, Saul tells his son Jonathan that by siding with David, he was forfeiting the kingdom Saul was seeking to pass on to him. In Saul's view, Jonathan was heir to his kingdom. Someone should have asked Saul, "Shall you decide who will be Israel's king? The kingdom is God's, not yours, and it is His decision who will rule!" No matter how badly Saul may have wanted Jonathan to rule after him, it was not his to decide. This intention of Saul's—to establish his descendants as Israel's monarchy by force—was very offensive to God. David's line was chosen instead. Later, when David set his son upon the throne, it was done according to God's revelation, not for his own continuation (1 Chron. 28:5–7).

It is very common in religion to assume that spiritual things can be passed on by way of inheritance. Many otherwise spiritual men have sought to find a place for their children in what the Lord has given them. Eli allowed his sons to serve as priests when they were not worthy (1 Sam. 2:22), and even Samuel attempted to set his sons up to govern Israel after him, in spite of the fact they did not know the Lord and even took bribes (1 Sam. 8:1–3). Samuel seemed to be perfect in every way except this. How difficult it is for a father not to want to see his son follow in his footsteps!

It is too easy to think that the Lord's ministry can be inherited. The ministry that the Lord has committed to a person operates as long as that person is present, but when that person dies, that ministry stops with him. Even if he wants to pass it on, he cannot. It is up to the Lord to raise up another minister to work with Him. In his book, *A Table in the Wilderness* (December 31st), Watchman Nee speaks of this, saying that once a servant of the Lord has served his generation and has passed on, the Lord must plow up everything to open the ground for whatever He will do next. In our concept, perhaps, it should be something carried on by way of inheritance, as a direct continuation. Such a notion is something of religion and hinders God from being the preeminent One among us.

Summoning Samuel through a Medium

The Philistines had come against Israel, and Saul brought his army up against them (1 Sam. 28:1, 4). Saul's heart "trembled

greatly" when he faced their army. Samuel, the person he depended upon to contact God, had passed away (v. 3). So what
did Saul do? He sought the help of a witch to bring Samuel back
from the dead! Saul simply did not know God, even though it
was God who had made him king. He knew enough to order
that all such spiritualists should be done away with in Israel, but
when he found himself in this situation, he himself used one
of them! Apparently he was surrounded by people who were
familiar with such evil things, for one of his servants knew of a
woman in En Dor who was a medium or witch. Saul disguised
himself and journeyed in the night with two others to consult
this medium. How low Saul had fallen! When he met her, she
was not easily persuaded to do what he wanted her to do, because he himself had commanded that all those who practiced
such things should be put to death. How did she know that they
were not spies of Saul?

Saul even swore to her by the Lord that no harm would come
to her if she did what he asked. In the name of the Lord, he, the
king of God's people, made a pact with a witch who worked with
God's enemy! So the woman did what he asked and summoned
up Samuel. When Samuel actually appeared, she was shocked,
for at that moment she realized that the person asking her to do
this could be none other than Saul himself.

When Saul asked what she saw, she replied that she saw a
spirit coming up out of the earth. It must have been something
to cause wonder. She described its appearance as an old man
wrapped in a mantle. Saul perceived that it must be Samuel and
bowed himself to the ground.

Samuel, however, rebuked Saul, saying, "Why have you
disturbed me by bringing me up?" (v. 15). Saul replied that he
was distressed because of the Philistines, and needed Samuel's
help. Saul was in a hopeless and helpless state—he had an enemy,
but he had no God, and no one who could communicate with
God for him. Therefore, he felt compelled to seek out a ghost!

Saul's experience could apply to us today. If we do not experience a living Christ, one day we may find ourselves standing be-
side the grave of a Christian we used to look up to. Some visit the

graves of spiritual men, and though they are not able to call these men up, they feel comforted telling the dead one the problems they seem unable to tell God. May the Lord preserve us from such an end. How we need to know the living Christ today!

We should practice to know the Lord and to have His presence in big and small matters—our education, our work, our career, our marriage, our family, whatever we face. Tell the Lord, "I do not want to end up praying at someone's tomb; I want to learn to know You as my Lord in everything. Lord, I want to have Your speaking for the rest of my life." We each must experience Jesus as our living Lord.

Samuel's Reaction

Samuel told Saul he could do nothing for him, saying, "The Lord has departed from you and has become your enemy....The Lord has torn the kingdom out of your hand and given it to your neighbor, David" (1 Sam. 28:16–17). Samuel had loved and even mourned over Saul, but since he was unable to help Saul while he was alive, Samuel certainly could do nothing more for Saul now that he was dead.

The Slippery Slope of Religion

Because of his religious nature, Saul had been sliding lower and lower. His religious nature caused him to offer without God (1 Sam. 13). Next, his religious nature caused him to feel he could make up for it by offering what God had condemned (1 Sam. 15). Then, Saul's religious nature brought him to the point that he only cared for the continuation of his own monarchy (1 Sam. 18, 20). Finally, his religious nature brought Saul to the point that he sought advice from a ghost through a witch (1 Sam. 28)! We now see someone far from the presence of God. Religion can degrade us to such an extent that we even get involved in things such as this. Once we get involved with religion, we have no idea how far it will eventually take us from God. This is why I refuse to compromise when I see anything coming in that might become a substitute for Christ, regardless how good or necessary it may seem. Though it be called a "top truth," a "top ministry," or even a "top oneness," if the believers are not brought to Christ Himself, it is vanity. Anything that is apart from Christ Himself cannot result in what is according to God's heart. The only thing that will be produced out of such things is another denomination.

4

David's Approvedness— Chosen, Anointed, Trained, and Tested

After considering Saul's experience, we might feel there is no escaping the slippery slope of religion. God, however, has given us a way. Saul's life is a warning to us. Now another person reveals what God is after. In David we see that God Himself is our way.

Chosen unto a Destiny

Before God could gain David, David had to experience a number of things. First, he was chosen by God from among his brothers, which was confirmed through Samuel (1 Sam. 16:10–12).

According to the apostle Paul, God chose us in Christ before the foundation of the world, having predestined us to be His sons (Eph. 1:4–5). Before anything existed, we were already chosen in Christ. The destiny decided for us beforehand was that we would be God's sons. Paul's realization was that he had been separated unto the Lord from his mother's womb (Gal. 1:15). This should be our realization as well. We are different from everyone else, for we have been chosen by God.

Unlike God's choosing, being chosen in our human life does not automatically ensure our achieving the goal for which we were chosen. For instance, when I went to Taiwan University, I was among 180 students chosen for our proficiency in English. A selection board chose us but was unable to predestinate us.

Thus, very few of us made much of a mark in the world. Our being chosen meant we could enter that school, but there was no guarantee that we would pass our classes, graduate from the program, or have a successful career. But God chose with a predestination! Our predetermined destiny is to be conformed to the image of the Lord Jesus Christ (Rom. 8:29). We were predestinated unto divine sonship!

Reaching the goal God has prepared for us, however, needs our participation. To be chosen is one thing, but to fulfill the purpose for our selection is another. Therefore, as those chosen by God we should not allow God's selection of us to be in vain (Phil. 2:12–13, 16; 2 Pet. 1:10). As those who have been selected by God we should pray, "Lord, I am here to participate in whatever You have prepared for me. It is my desire to be faithful to Your selection."

Chosen

After God commanded Samuel to stop mourning for Saul, whom He had rejected, He sent him to anoint another king from among the sons of Jesse the Bethlehemite (1 Sam. 16:1). Samuel feared Saul would kill him if he found out the reason for his journey. Therefore, God told him to say he was going in order to offer a sacrifice. After he arrived at Jesse's home, he invited Jesse and his sons to the sacrifice.

This picture should impress us. Like David, we are being called to something so high, but we must also realize that we are being called to an altar of sacrifice. If we desire to be useful to the Lord, we must be prepared to become a sacrifice, having no rights or freedom to do our own things. Once we become a sacrifice, anything we had as a life outside of God is finished.

Samuel may have hoped that God would choose Eliab, the oldest son, for he looked very promising. However, God told Samuel not to be impressed with Eliab's stature and appearance, for He looked not at the outward appearance, but on the heart (1 Sam. 16:7). We should aspire to have a heart that would allow

God to choose us. Samuel called the next son, and the next, until he had seen seven of Jesse's sons. Samuel said, "The Lord has not chosen these" (v. 10). Jesse indicated he had one more son, the youngest, but he was watching the sheep. Therefore, Jesse sent for David, who must have been some distance away. Samuel said that no one would sit down to eat until the matter was accomplished, so they all waited solemnly.

Anointed

When David was finally brought before them, Samuel saw that he was "ruddy, with bright eyes, and good-looking" (1 Sam. 16:12). The Lord told Samuel, "Arise, anoint him, for this is the one!" Therefore Samuel took the horn of oil he was commanded to bring and anointed David in the midst of his brothers. From that day forward, the Bible tells us that David had the Spirit of the Lord upon him (v. 13).

David was chosen and anointed. These are two different things. As believers, we have been chosen from among all the other people before the foundation of the world. Before anything else existed, God chose us and even marked us out for His satisfaction (Eph. 1:4–5). Then we are anointed. The anointing David received is a picture of the New Testament believers' experience of the Spirit (Acts 10:38; 2 Cor. 1:21). Therefore, we should seek to live and walk in the Spirit continually (Gal. 5:25). If we are faithful to follow the Lord who chose us, our experience of the anointing Spirit will become more substantial. The apostle John describes the assurance the Spirit brings: "By this we know that we abide in Him, and He in us, because He has given us of His Spirit" (1 John 4:13).

The experience of the Spirit can be inward (John 20:22) or outward (Acts 10:45). We can pray to the extent that we are filled with the Spirit. Sometimes when believers pray together and claim the efficacy of the Lord's blood, sing a chorus of a hymn, and continue to pray until their spirits are elevated, they experience the Spirit's filling. For one person to seek this

individually is difficult, but I hope many would gather in such a
way to practice entering into the Lord's presence.

A Personal Testimony

My experience of the Spirit somewhat matches that of Tim-
othy (1 Tim. 4:14; 2 Tim. 1:6). I received the Lord when I was
in high school. I began to read the Bible, preach the gospel, and
serve in the church life. I became known as a crazy Jesus-lover.
Everyone at school knew that I was on fire for Jesus Christ. It
may seem like that would have been enough to satisfy my desire to serve the Lord, but eventually I felt strongly constrained
to give my life to Him completely. I shared this desire with the
elders. That Saturday night there was a meeting, and they asked
me to testify how I wanted to live for Christ and Christ alone.
After reading a letter of consecration I had written and giving
my testimony, I knelt down, and four elders of the church laid
their hands on me. At that time I experienced what Psalm 133
mentions about the Lord's anointing descending from on high.
I began to weep so strongly that I could not stand. Others had
to lift me up and walk me to my seat. I could not stop weeping
until the following day. I was so touched by the Lord's love. I
believe it was as the verses that say, "The love of Christ compels
us..." (2 Cor. 5:14–15). I felt that the Lord was so good, so
lovely, and so precious. I became a different person. I became
so bold before God and man. After I experienced the Lord's
anointing in this way, I felt like the happiest person on the
globe, for at that moment God and I were totally one.

Of course, it has taken me fifty years to apply what I experienced on that day. It was not simply a "one-time deal."
David, after his anointing, experienced the Spirit being with
him all his days. I hope that everyone who has received Christ
as their Savior would go on to experience the Spirit. Go before the Lord even for a number of hours to confess any sins
or shortcomings as He reveals them to you, and ask Him to
fill you. Tell Him you need His Spirit to saturate you so you

might become an anointed person. I do not want to promote a specific way, but every Christian needs to experience the Spirit. The experience of being anointed is something of the operation of the Spirit upon you which sets you apart unto God for His purpose.

Trained

Although David didn't realize it at the time, his experience as a shepherd was part of his training to be king. David was the only king of Israel who was called as a shepherd. He used many of the principles he learned as a shepherd to rule over God's flock.

When I traveled to Inner Mongolia, I went to see the vast grasslands. I saw a large flock of sheep being watched over by a man and his dog. The sheep dog was very busy, running to and fro to keep the sheep where the man wanted them. Gradually, as the sheep finished eating the grass in one area, the man moved them on to a new pasture. Most of the time, however, the shepherd simply sat and watched the sheep. David developed in this way. His training was hands on, not theoretical. He developed the ability to patiently watch over the flock and the surrounding environment. He composed Psalm 8 based on his long nights watching the sheep, considering the heavens, and wondering about God. Night and day, he had to be on guard against any beasts that might try to steal one of the sheep. This would explain why he was such an expert with his sling when he faced Goliath (1 Sam. 17:36). Since he was responsible for the flock, he did not run from the bear or the lion. He faced them, and as he triumphed over them he discovered how faithful God was to watch over him and his sheep (v. 37). This training qualified him to rule over Israel as God's flock. In Psalm 23, he records the lessons he learned while shepherding. Whatever challenged his flock, whether beast, Philistine, or strong nation, he stood firm. The Lord was the real Shepherd over both him and the nation of Israel.

Willing to Be Trained

How should we be trained? Begin by being faithful to the seemingly little thing that is now in your hand, whatever it may be. The flock David's father gave him to watch over was small (1 Sam. 17:28), yet David was faithful to his charge. We like prestigious assignments, but if we cannot give ourselves to what is already in our hands, we are not going to be able to carry anything greater. David was charged to watch those few sheep; his life was linked to theirs as long as he was their shepherd. That is why he was strong to defend them. If he had despised his assignment or had been careless in carrying it out, he would not have been bold to engage Goliath or the other enemies that threatened God's flock. A person with an indifferent attitude cannot carry God's commitment.

Many resist giving themselves to be trained. If we are not trained, however, even though we may be very gifted, we will not accomplish for God what we might have. I am always impressed with people who have musical talent. Some can play piano by ear without any formal training. They can play beautiful music, yet without training their ability to develop any further is limited. If they wish to discover their real potential, they need to be trained.

Twenty years from now, the untrained person will not have become useful to the Lord. They may be captured by their careers or families, or may just come to nothing. They may become churchgoers with no real heart for what God is after. However, those who are willing to be trained by being faithful to what the Lord has committed to them will become those God is seeking after, those who are after His heart.

When I began to love the Lord, the first thing He told me to do was to take care of the children in the church. Therefore, for ten years, while I was in high school, the military, and college, I taught children the Bible. This is one reason I know the Old Testament as well as I do. I am very glad that I was able to serve in that capacity for all those years. As a young believer, I received my training by serving children.

Today I am seventy, but I do not feel old, for I have been bearing the Lord's commitment, and I am still bearing it. Even at my age, there is more and more to be done for the Lord's interest. Our labor can have eternal value. How high is such a life! I hope many who read this would determine, "I may be young in the Lord, but something of eternal value will be manifested through me! What I am giving myself to will be manifested in eternity! I am a person in time, but what I am doing is unto eternity!"

Tested

Immediately after he was anointed, David entered a long period of testing. He was not instantly recognized as the new king. Saul remained as king. However, the Spirit of the Lord departed from Saul, and a distressing spirit troubled him. Saul's servants suggested that a skillful harp player could make Saul well at such times, so David was called in to play (1 Sam. 16:14–23). David, knowing that he was anointed to be king, served Saul and did what he could for him. He played his harp to soothe Saul and also became his armorbearer. Someone in David's position might have been tempted to allow the evil spirit to do its work of tormenting Saul. Though David was anointed to be king after Saul, he did nothing to hasten Saul's downfall; instead, he served and honored him.

The Lord allows things to happen to us so that we may grow. If we never experienced difficulties or failures, our training might make us appear to be very prevailing when in fact we are not experiencing anything real. Therefore, God does not always allow things to go smoothly for us. When difficulties came to David, he trusted the Lord and rested in Him. As David played his harp to soothe Saul, he knew that the Lord was at work to carry out what He desired for him. We all should be able to tell the Lord, "I know everything is in Your hands," and be restful.

When I look back, I have to marvel. Immediately after my

experience of the Spirit when the elders laid their hands on me, I began to seek the Lord regarding where I should go to college. I wrongly assumed I would never be qualified to attend Taiwan University. One day, as I rode my bike past Normal College, I asked the Lord to please send me to that school. I was indeed admitted there, but only into the Boy Scout program, a two-year program with no degree. The Lord gave me what I asked for, but I realized I had not specified which program I wanted. Therefore, I took the university examination again and this time qualified for Taiwan University. There was a bureaucratic mix-up, however, and my name was overlooked. My father, who was a general, went in and demanded that the wrong be righted, but it was too late; I had to take the test once more! This time, I took the test with my brother, who was five years younger than I. We knew someone who could notify us of our score a day before the public posting, so we waited by the phone at the arranged time. I answered it when it rang, and the person on the other end said, "Congratulations to your brother! He made it into Taiwan University." I then asked, "How about me?" He responded, "You were one point short." At that moment I saw how real God was. My mother was upset at my failure, so the whole family had to act disappointed. However, I was rejoicing and singing songs to the Lord. My mother asked why I was so happy, and I told her that it was because the Lord was with me.

I was allowed into an officers' language school to learn English even though I was only a high school graduate. For one year, I worked as an interpreter for American officers before I entered college. The Lord used this to prepare me to serve Him in the United States. I had no plan to come to the USA, yet He put me into a military language school to learn English whether I wanted to or not. I became, in fact, the English interpreter for my own father—just consider how enjoyable that was! Therefore, when a time of testing comes, do not be discouraged, for there is nothing to be discouraged about. The Lord is at work. We all must appreciate the times of testing, for they are precious.

Purity and View

Two major items that the Lord tests are our purity and our view. This was David's experience. He became the prevailing warrior in the kingdom, outshining Saul, yet he carried Saul's armor. David still honored Saul as God's anointed. David's view was that, since God anointed him, he would stand with him. If David had a natural view, he would have sought to hasten Saul's death to make it clear who the Lord's anointed was. All David had to do, it seemed, was to refuse to play his harp for Saul, for then the evil spirit might have driven him mad or caused him to kill himself. If David simply had the throne in view, he might have done such a thing, but David was very pure. In his view, since God had anointed him, God was responsible for his kingship to be manifest. David did not have to do anything on his own behalf. This is not an easy lesson to learn.

We live before God according to our purity, and we live among men according to our view. Our purity decides how well we grow before God and how well we are able to understand spiritual things. Our view decides our manner of life among men and how we operate in this life (Prov. 23:7). When we are one with God, our view will be one with God's view. If we are thinking the same way that God is thinking, then we are people touching God's heart.

Manifested through Testing

We often find it difficult to pass through times of testing because such testing seems unreasonable. We may find ourselves put aside and even blockaded by someone. Instead of having the opportunity to show what we are capable of doing, it seems we become stuck in a place where we are never appreciated. Yet we must pass through these times of testing before we can be approved (1 Thess. 2:4; 1 Pet. 1:7).

Instead of complaining about the elders, feeling they are incompetent for not putting our talent to use, we should realize that the Lord is not making a mistake. Every spiritual thing we think we possess has to be tested to see if it is real. Therefore, not only must we be chosen, anointed, and trained, but we must also be tested. Many who love the Lord simply cannot make it through the period of testing that leads to approvedness.

I know a Christian brother who moved to the United States and was made an elder in a large church. Others heard of this and moved to the same area, thinking they might also be appointed to leadership positions. When this didn't happen, they got disappointed and eventually moved back. Testing is not easy! If the Lord leads you to move somewhere, go with no expectations other than to find the Lord Himself. Many who think they have something expect to be appreciated and put to use so that they might do great things. They feel ready and think, "Aren't I more capable than those who are already serving? Why don't they recognize who I am and what I can do? Oh, if only those who are blocking me would step aside and give me a chance!" The Lord just doesn't seem to cooperate; He allows this situation to manifest what is in your heart.

If you feel others are in your way, you are looking at things as though you are in an institution, not the Lord's organic body. Rather, you should stand with those you think are in your way. Serve with them and help them! Do this and you will become fruitful. You will find you possess approvedness. However, if you just feel blocked, you will not find approvedness no matter how trained you are. You will wonder why others seem cold toward you. Actually, they are not the problem. The whole situation is to test you. Only through such testing will you find opportunities to be approved.

Approved

Saul and the armies of Israel, including David's three oldest brothers, were in battle array against the attacking Philistines. Goliath, a giant among the Philistines, challenged any Israelite to fight him. At this point, David was sent to the battlefront by his father to bring supplies to his brothers and to bring back word how things were going (1 Sam. 17:17–18). Upon arriving, he found Goliath mocking Israel and Saul hiding in his tent, considering how to save himself, his army, and the country. Why didn't Saul at least order his archers to shoot down Goliath? If David could kill him by striking him in the forehead with a stone, couldn't an archer have struck him down while he was mocking God and His people? Yet it seems that among all the Israelites, only David was upset that Goliath was allowed to defy the armies of the living God (v. 26). To David, the people of Israel were not simply Israelites; they were the people whose God was the living God. Where were those among His people who would challenge these idol worshipers on behalf of the true and living God?

David was God's anointed. To his brothers, however, he was just a little boy who had sneaked away from his duties at home to see the battle. David's brothers were probably not too happy that Samuel had anointed him instead of one of them. Furthermore, it probably annoyed them when he asked why no one was going out to defeat Goliath. His oldest brother said, "I know why you are here. You just want to be where the action is." Yet David answered, "Is there not a cause?" (1 Sam. 17:29). David knew there was a reason for his coming at that specific time. He was God's anointed, and his being there meant something. He had an inner realization that God had sent him for this very purpose.

Like David, we should also be able to recognize when such a time arrives. It is not unusual for people to act cowardly as the Israelites did in this situation. If, however, the Lord has revealed something to us, shouldn't we have the same boldness as David? We should be able to say, "Is there not a cause for our being here at this moment? We are here for the testimony of the Lord Jesus Christ!" David testified to Saul that the Lord had delivered him from the paw of the bear and the lion, and that the Lord would deliver him out of the hand of the Philistine giant (1 Sam. 17:36–37). In the past, David had seen how the Lord had been his protection and realized that the Lord was still his protection. David was confident that the Lord would be with him in this fight.

Using His Sling rather than Saul's Armor

Saul offered David his armor, but David ultimately refused it (1 Sam. 17:38–39). He fought according to who he was as a shepherd and used the sling and stones he knew. The secret of fighting is not to borrow from others but to use what we ourselves have learned and applied. You may repeat someone else's teaching—there is nothing wrong with that—but if you want to war the genuine warfare, what you wield has to be something that comes from you. Saul's armor might have been of use if David was only interested in protecting himself, but his intention was to attack the enemy, not to set up a defense. When David went out to meet Goliath, he carried no protection; he just went out. In his mind there was only, "Either he dies, or I die." David was not interested in self-preservation; his desire was to see God's testimony lifted up on the earth.

If we are after the Lord's heart, when the time comes to fight, we will not consider how to protect ourselves or our interests; our only desire will be to see that the Lord's interest is cared for. We all should be so firm when it comes to this matter.

The Shepherd Boy Kills the Philistine Dog

Goliath mocked when he saw David with his staff and sling, saying, "Am I a dog, that you come to me with sticks?" (1 Sam. 17:43). David was probably used to fighting wild dogs and jackals as he guarded his father's sheep. Since such animals attacked in packs, David would have learned to attack them before they could set themselves. David probably thought to himself, "You are right. I deal with dogs like you all the time." He then killed him with one stone from his sling, winning a great victory for Israel. Saul greatly appreciated David at this point and eventually set him over all his men of war (1 Sam. 18:5). David's approvedness among the people, however, earned him Saul's suspicion. After Saul heard how the women praised

David more than they praised him, Saul began to look upon David as a threat (1 Sam. 18:6–9).

David's approvedness introduced him to a life under persecution. Saul tried to kill David, took his wife from him, and even hunted for him after he fled to the wilderness. During the years David was fleeing from Saul, many dispossessed and hopeless people came to him. He worked with them and formed them into a loyal and effective fighting force. David provides us one of the best examples in the Bible of what it means to be chosen, anointed, trained, tested, and eventually approved.

5

Learning to Trust
Only God

Having been chosen, anointed, trained, tested, and approved, David was greatly appreciated by Saul. David became exceptionally manifest among God's people. His victories in battle won him public praise. Once the king's armorbearer, David now ranked among the few men who sat with Saul, and he became the king's son-in-law by marrying his daughter, Michal. Even though David was still a young man, Saul set him over the men of war (1 Sam. 18:5). David behaved wisely and had the presence of the Lord (v. 14). He was surely held in high regard and appreciated by everyone.

Aspire to Be Manifested

As believers, we should seek manifestation. Even young people should have such an aspiration. We should not be overly concerned whether or not this desire is from our soul-life. We should fight to make our mark before the Lord and then let the Lord work on us. We should experience fruit from our gospel preaching; we should see impact when we share; and we should be appreciated by others in the church, including the more experienced ones. All these are experiences of being manifested. When we have such experiences, we must tell the Lord, "I am not for this, I am for You. My desire in all this is to carry out what is in Your heart." The Lord must be our center. He alone must become the reality of our living, our serving, and our daily

labor. We should not be content to simply become good, functioning members in the church life. No! We should fight to have
something extra before the Lord. We should desire to become a
blessing to the Lord, the church, and the believers we are with.
Such an aspiration is precious. If we lack the experience of being manifested, we will lack what has been given to sustain us
during the periods of difficulty and hardship.

The Women's Praise

Once, when David and Saul were returning from battle, the
women came forth to sing their praises using tambourines and
other instruments of music. This must have been a wonderful
and joyous sight. They exalted David as the greatest fighter
in Israel, even above Saul, singing, "Saul has slain his thousands, and David his ten thousands" (1 Sam. 18:7). If only they
had praised God instead of David, he would have been spared
much suffering.

Many Christians exalt people instead of simply lifting up
the Lord. This always leads to problems. The women's excessive
praise of David stirred Saul to jealousy, ushering in the next
phase of David's development—the persecution from Saul. The
early period of manifestation was only the flowering stage; now,
during the time of David's sufferings, he would grow into a
mighty tree.

Seeking Refuge

The first thing the Lord dealt with in His deeper work was
David's dependence upon persons and things. The Lord wanted
David to depend upon Himself alone. Saul's jealousy caused
him to try to kill David. Twice Saul personally tried to kill him
by throwing his spear at him (1 Sam. 18:11; 19:9–10) and then
had his men try to kill him in his own home (1 Sam 19:11).
David had to flee for his life.

The first person David ran to was Samuel. The Lord had used Samuel to anoint David, but David had to learn that if he relied upon Samuel, he would be in trouble when Samuel was gone. Next, he went to his closest companion, Saul's son Jonathan. Jonathan loved him but could not become David's refuge in time of trouble. David then visited the priests of Nob, but both he and they realized he could not stay there. They gave him bread for his journey—an act they later paid for dearly—but they could not shelter him. David then fled for refuge outside the land of Israel to King Achish of the Philistines. Here he was compelled to act insane because they found out who he was.

Seeking Refuge with Samuel

Saul told Jonathan his son and all his servants that they were to kill David, but Jonathan persuaded his father to spare him (1 Sam. 19:1–6). Later, when David returned from another great victory over the Philistines, he again played his harp to relieve Saul of the distressing spirit from the Lord (vv. 8–9). As David played, Saul took up his spear and threw it at him, but David escaped and fled. Jealousy is terrible. When we hear someone give a good message, we may be stung by jealousy. If we hear someone else being complimented for something, we may be bitten by jealousy.

When David fled from Saul, he went to his house. Saul sent messengers to watch for him and kill him in the morning. David's wife, Michal, warned him of their plot and let him down through a window so that he might escape (1 Sam. 19:12). She put an image in the bed in place of David and a cover of goat's hair where his head would have been. Why did David have an image in his home? In the Bible, such images are forbidden and usually are idols. It seems that a thing that God hates was used to save David's life.

David fled to Samuel (1 Sam. 19:18). When Saul heard this, he sent messengers to seize David. When they arrived, they met a company of prophets led by Samuel. The Spirit of God came upon the messengers, and they began prophesying also! Perhaps they prophesied that David would become king. Saul, of course, was more upset than ever. He sent another group of messengers who also began to prophesy with the group of prophets. Saul sent a third group, and the same thing happened again. You have to love the Lord for His way of handling things. Not only is He powerful, wise, and lovely, but He is so humorous. How glorious and wonderful it is to follow Him!

Finally, Saul chose to go himself. David must have been trembling, for he had no army. When Saul arrived, probably with a number of his officers, he too experienced what the others had, but even more so, for not only did he prophesy, he even stripped naked and lay on the ground, prophesying for an entire day and night (1 Sam. 19:23–24). Although God delivered David in such a miraculous way, David had not yet fully learned to trust God for his protection. He might have looked over at Samuel and asked, "Why did you take me away from watching my sheep? What have you gotten me into?" Wouldn't things have gone much easier for David if God simply removed Saul in some way? Why does God have to make things so complicated?

When I consider this picture, I have to laugh and say, "Lord, I cannot but love You. No one is as wise as You." God was training David to depend upon no one but Himself. It was as if He were saying, "Samuel may have anointed you, and he may be judge, priest, and prophet, but do not trust in him. You must trust in Me." These experiences of persecution were to teach David that only God could be relied upon. Although David had trusted God as he confronted the bear, the lion, Goliath, and the armies of the Philistines, his flight to Samuel showed he still had more to learn. As Saul sought to kill David, God was teaching David to rely wholly upon Himself.

David must have felt a real sense of relief every time he was delivered, yet that cycle of events must have been very scary. Therefore, David left Samuel and went to Jonathan, his close friend.

Seeking Help from Jonathan

The Bible tells us that Jonathan loved David as his own soul (1 Sam. 18:1). Jonathan did not care whether or not he would become king. He was pure. He seemed happy that David would become king instead of him (23:16–17).

In chapter twenty, I believe the primary reason David went to Jonathan was to discover if Saul had any change of heart after prophesying under the Spirit's power. If I had been Saul, I surely would have returned and reconsidered the whole thing. He should have realized that all his struggling against David was foolish. So many people struggle to make it to the top, to get the best grades, and the best paying career, but in the final analysis, they should learn that such struggles in the absence of God are vain. David was winning victories for Israel, was very faithful to Saul, and had never done anything rebellious. Saul should have realized that it was up to God to chose who would be the next king, whether it be Jonathan, David, or someone else. Therefore, David went to Jonathan to see if his father had experienced such a change of heart. Jonathan informed David that his father indeed seemed to have had such a change. Just to be sure, they agreed that David would not sit at the king's table that night to see how Saul would react. When Saul discovered David's absence, he was enraged. Jonathan let David know his father's reaction and said what must have felt like their final good-byes (1 Sam. 20:42).

Receiving the Showbread from the Priests

As David was fleeing from Saul, he sought help from the priests of Nob. They gave him the holy showbread to eat which was supposed to be only for the priests (1 Sam. 21:1–6; Matt. 12:3–4). If Saul had eaten this bread, it seems it would have been counted against him. Yet because it was David who ate it, God seemed very happy. The priests could not shelter David, however, because they all realized Saul was now tormented by an evil spirit and driven by jealousy to destroy David, whatever the cost.

Because the priests of Nob had sustained David with some of the holy showbread, Saul had the entire village of priests destroyed (1 Sam. 22: 11–19). Only one priest, Abiathar, was able to escape. At one time, Saul had been good, but this time, he had become a different person. That is why he could carry out such an atrocity. Because of a few loaves of bread, he slaughtered eighty-five priests, along with the entire town of Nob, including men, women, and children. He did not even spare the infants. How could one who had been anointed by God become so evil? Remember, Saul became who he was due to religion. Let this become a warning to us, for the hatred generated by religion far exceeds the hatred generated by other matters. In politics, for example, opponents can still shake hands and respect one another. In religion, however, a man may hate his opponent beyond all reason. As lovers of Jesus, how careful we must be not to become involved in religion! Those we trust can utterly betray us. We must be aware that such things can happen. This has become the testimony of many of the great servants of the Lord.

Seeking Refuge among the Philistines

David left God's people and fled to Gath, one of the main cities in the land of the Philistines (1 Sam. 21:10). The servants of Achish, the king of Gath, had heard of David and told Achish, "Is this not David the king of the land? Did they not sing of him to one another in dances, saying: 'Saul has slain his thousands, and David his ten thousands'?" (v. 11). The trouble the women had begun in Israel with Saul now reached even to the Gentile lands. If Christians would only learn not to exalt one servant of the Lord above another, there would be much more peace among God's people.

Therefore, David was in trouble again. If he could have lived unrecognized among the Philistines, he might have dwelt among them in peace. Even in the Gentile world, David was too famous. This was not a blessing. It forced David to change his behavior. He feigned insanity. He let saliva fall upon his beard, and scratched meaninglessly at the doors of the gate, leading the Philistines to believe he had gone mad (1 Sam. 21:13–14). This story illustrates that we cannot expect to find refuge in the world, for to survive and be accepted in the world requires us to live a life that is not right.

Finding Refuge in the Cave of Adullam

David was able to escape the situation in Gath because of his feigned madness. Realizing that there was no one left to protect him, he took refuge in the cave of Adullam (1 Sam. 22:1). Like David, we believers all pass through various experiences until we finally discover that only God is our true refuge. While David was in this cave, his father's household came to him (v. 1). All his brothers came to stand with him. This must have been a real comfort to David. Also, all those who were distressed, in debt, and discontented came to him and took him as their captain (v. 2). In other words, the homeless and unwanted came to David. None of the thousands of troops he commanded came to him nor any of those women who sang his praises. Instead, those who came were the psychologically distressed, those unable to hold down a job, and those who could find no satisfaction in their current situation.

Forging an Army out of the Hopeless

About four hundred hopeless men gathered themselves to David, and he began to form them into his army (1 Sam. 22:2). God sent these men to David, and he did not complain. Whenever Saul found someone who was valiant or mighty, he took that person to himself (14:52). David, however, didn't do this. He received and trained all who came to him. If I had been David, I might said, "Please God, I don't want to run a refugee camp or treatment center. What are You doing to me by sending me all these problem cases?" But David was not like this. Once these hopeless men came to David, he took them in, fed them, and worked with them. He felt responsible for them. Perhaps he felt, "Although others might see these men as problem cases, after I live and work with them, everyone will be surprised at the potential of these men God gave me and what they have become." Unlike Saul, who recruited all the strongest and most valiant men in Israel, David took those the Lord sovereignly sent to him.

Therefore, David became the captain of these four hundred men. I believe that the group who were later called David's mighty men came from this first group of seemingly hopeless cases. In our church life, we should learn this lesson. We shouldn't try to recruit those who seem more promising than others; instead, we should receive those the Lord sends us.

As we consider the individuals who have gathered unto the Lord in our church, we might feel we are a hopeless group. Yet in a similar circumstance, David was able to form the people into a prevailing fighting force. We can rest assured that there is nothing wrong with those the Lord has brought together in our church. They may appear peculiar and have defects, but this is not the issue. The real issue is whether we know how to work with those the Lord has brought together. Even though David himself seemed hopeless, having lost everything and living as an exile in a cave, he was very clear he was still God's anointed. This caused him to realize that no one is hopeless. God could work with anyone, including the four hundred who gathered around him. It is crucial for us to realize this also.

False Expectations

Many believers today are like the men who gathered to David: discontented, distressed, and in debt. Just about every person who gets saved does so under the false impression that freedom from everything negative will immediately follow.

Furthermore, just about every person who gets saved does so for selfish reasons—to go to heaven, not hell. Every believer was told that Jesus would cancel the debt of sin and immediately remove its power. While it is true that Jesus took away the debt of sin, our subjective experience of its power over us still remains. Therefore, nearly everyone who gets regenerated ends up feeling like the wretched man of Romans chapter seven (v. 24) who finds himself still under the control of indwelling sin (vv. 19–20). What a paradox! The church life is filled with such distressed people.

When I was first saved, I was asked to fill out a questionnaire to determine my understanding of the Christian faith. I was happy to answer questions such as, "Do you believe in Jesus?" "Is Jesus God?" "Is the Bible the Word of God?" and so on. It seemed that all the questions should be answered with a "yes." When I arrived at the question, "Will you sin again?" I thought, "The preacher said no more sin," so I wrote, "No." We are funny people. Either we proclaim we are able to follow the Lord victoriously when, in fact, we cannot, or we despise ourselves and seek refuge in a worldly life.

From Malcontents to Mighty Men

God's intention in saving us is not merely to rescue us from hell but that we might be one with Him for His purpose. God wants a people who are after His own heart, one with Him, ready to fight for His kingdom.

Only malcontents came to David, yet he was able to train them all. These became the base of his strength by which he raised up Judah and eventually all the kingdom of Israel. None of them were people of note. They were not graduates from the best universities, or the brightest stars in Israel. Therefore, tell those who are caring for you, "Please don't say I am no good. I am in distress, in debt, and discontented. Train me that I might be a mighty man in God's army!" (See 2 Sam. 10:7; 23:8.) Such a group formed the core of David's kingdom.

Isn't this encouraging? It was not those who seemed promising that David used to form the nucleus of his kingdom. It was those who were like us, those who were struggling just to make it.

You may feel you are in distress, in debt, or discontented, yet regardless of your feeling, you are qualified to be trained by the Lord Jesus Christ. He will receive you, and, if you allow Him, He will make you a mighty man able to fight for the sake of His kingdom.

David in the Cave—Psalm 34

The Chinese Bible says that David wrote Psalm 34 while he was in the cave of Adullam, which followed his experience with King Achish. In that cave, David had nothing to look at but a stone floor, a stone ceiling, and stone walls. When he was a shepherd, at least he could look up at the sky. Wouldn't it have seemed a good time for David to complain at least a little bit? Yet he did not write to bemoan his situation or all he had lost. He could have written about how he had been riding on a great white stallion at the front of a vast army and how he was now training four hundred misfits hiding in a cave. He also could have lamented over how foolish the women had been to stir up Saul's jealousy with their singing. Instead he wrote,

I will bless the Lord at all times;
His praise shall continually be in my mouth.

David's boast was not that he had killed Goliath, that he had married Michal, that the women of Israel had endorsed him, or that as a young man he had surpassed many much older than he. I believe David's feeling was, "How glorious it is that I have followed the Lord. What a wonderful decision!" Before this time, David was too busy to boast in anything, for he was making himself manifest for the Lord's sake. That was right and proper, for without that manifestation, the Lord would have never been able to bring David to this point. Now the Lord was stripping away these things to bring David down from such a height to such a depth. He had nothing outward left to boast in. He now could say with assurance,

My soul shall make its boast in the Lord.

He could have boasted in many things before, but now he had nothing to point to other than the Lord Himself. If he were to point somewhere in the cave, his finger would fall on one who was in distress, in debt, or discontented. Yet David could say to those around him,

Oh, magnify the Lord with me,
And let us exalt His name together.
I sought the Lord, and He heard me,
And delivered me from all my fears.

I am impressed with David. He was able to say that the Lord had delivered him from all his fears. This is meaningful, because God had not yet delivered David from those who sought his life. In fact, things seemed to be getting worse, not better! If someone were trying to kill you, it would seem logical to ask the Lord to deliver you from this one. Once you have been delivered from your fears, however, you are able to tell your enemy, "Who are you? Why should I be afraid of you?" As sons of God, we, like David, should be able to say, "The Lord has delivered me from all my fears!" Then, even if our enemies increase, we will still be able to rest. David was even able to say,

Oh, taste and see that the Lord is good;
Blessed is the man who trusts in Him!

David was saying, "Nothing and no one but God is worthy of my trust. I tried other means, but none satisfied. I have tasted and seen that the Lord is good. Only the Lord is able to be my salvation. Now my rest is in Him alone."

David also wrote,

The Lord is near to those who have a broken heart,
And saves such as have a contrite spirit.

When David was riding before a great army, praised and viewed as such a manifest champion of the Lord, he didn't know what it was to have a broken heart. By the time he reached the cave of Adullam, however, his suffering brought him this experience. Yet he could still praise the Lord and testify that the Lord was good. The two do not conflict. You can experience being broken-hearted and tasting the Lord's sweetness at the same time. Your spirit can be joyful, even as your soul suffers.

To be contrite means to be deeply sorrowful and repentant. I believe David had a realization of how proud and self-sufficient he had been during the period of his manifestation. He once was a powerful man enjoying success, but now he realized that God was his only means of survival. Therefore, he could say that the Lord was near to everyone who has a broken heart and saves such as have a spirit of deep repentance. David had so much to repent of, but he did not have time for regret. He was of a contrite spirit, and that was enough.

Delivering Keilah from the Philistines

It might have seemed good to David to remain in the cave in that state of repentance and reflection, all the while forming those who came to him into a fighting force. However, news came that the town of Keilah was under attack by the Philistines. David asked the Lord whether he should attack the marauding Philistines, and the Lord said to go up and deliver the town. Therefore, David and his men fought the Philistines and saved the inhabitants of the town, taking away the Philistines' livestock (1 Sam. 23:1–5).

At this point, Abiathar, the only priest who escaped Saul's slaughter of the priests at Nob, arrived (1 Sam. 23:6). What a blessing this was, for now there was a king and a priest who were able to serve together!

Escaping to the Wilderness

When Saul heard that David was in Keilah, he began to gather men to besiege the city. News of Saul's plan reached David, and he inquired of the Lord whether the people he had rescued would turn him over to Saul. The Lord told him they would (1 Sam. 23:10–12). This probably surprised David. Having just rescued the city, no doubt he hoped he and his men could stay there awhile instead of hiding in the cave. He even had a priest by his side, a clear sign that the Lord was with him. Yet at that moment, news of Saul came, and David found out that those he rescued could not be trusted; they would betray him. Therefore, David fled Keilah and made his abode in the strongholds in the wilderness. Those who serve the Lord may not necessarily have many good days. Eventually all that happened resulted in one thing: the realization that the Lord alone is trustworthy.

6

Forming the Nucleus Of His Kingdom— His Fighters

How was David able to take the group of hapless people God sent to him and form them into an army able to deliver the city of Keilah from the attacking Philistines? The number of people who first came to David was four hundred, but by the time he rescued Keilah, that number had grown to six hundred (1 Sam. 22:2; 23:13). This group became the nucleus of a prevailing army which fought alongside David for the establishment of his kingdom. Thirty-seven from among them became renowned as David's mighty men (2 Sam. 23:8–39). If you love the Lord, aspire to become such a "mighty man" in God's spiritual army. We are all qualified.

In order to produce such an army, David paid attention to four matters. First, he remained in the Lord's presence, learning to trust Him in all things, even in times of defeat. Second, he cared for those the Lord sent to him, investing himself in them. Third, he trained them to do as he did: to trust in God and invest themselves in others. Finally, he provided opportunities for them to use what they learned—a field to labor in.

Remaining in the Lord's Presence

David never dwelt in defeat. Though he confronted all kinds of difficulty and hardship, he never gave up. Even Elijah, one of the greatest prophets in the Old Testament, had times when he wanted to give up (1 Kings 19:2–4). David never acted this way, for he knew how to turn to the Lord and trust in Him, even in the midst of failure. Those who came to David must have been impressed by how he could write Psalm 34 while hiding in the cave of Adullam.

A person can fail without being defeated, just as a person can be defeated without having failed. The secret of never being defeated is to always have fresh experiences of Christ. Even in David's most abysmal failures, he still turned to the Lord. For example, after Nathan, the prophet, confronted David about his adulterous relationship with Bathsheba, David had a genuine repentance (Psalm 51). He never became so defeated that he even momentarily considered giving up the Lord.

There are multiple reasons why we might consider giving up the Lord. We might be caught by sin or worldliness, but the main reason is that the Lord no longer holds the first place in our heart. Too often we gauge our spiritual condition by how victorious we are, but David's measure was the Lord's presence. His secret was that he only wanted the Lord. Whether he was victorious or defeated, he sought the Lord's presence. This became the secret of everything he did from this time forward. We will experience both days of victory and days of defeat, but either way, we need to remain in the Lord's presence. No matter what we are going through, we need to remain with the Lord, learning to trust Him in all things.

Investing in Others

Saul recruited the most capable men for the sake of his kingdom (1 Sam. 14:52). For instance, if someone from Harvard had appeared, Saul might have recruited him for his education department. If he were to see a graduate from West Point, he would have asked him to fill some role in his military. Saul, however, used these recruits as mere instruments to reach his own goals. This was not David's way. He received and cared for all those the Lord sent him, investing himself in them. This is why it was such a great offense to God when David numbered the people, for in this instance, he was looking at them as mere capital (2 Sam. 24:2–17). When he realized what he had done by numbering the people, he immediately repented and turned back to the Lord. That was one of his biggest failings, for it was totally against what he stood for as a man after God's heart. He took care of those the Lord sent him. This was one reason David was able to raise them up.

We should see others in this way. We should never view others as a means of furthering our own interest. We will never fully mature if we do not know how to raise up others, just as people never fully mature until they become parents. As they help their children grow, they experience another stage of growth themselves. Those who do not invest themselves in others will never mature properly. Therefore, if you want to grow, invest yourself in somebody else. Though you may become a manifest leader in your church, you will not have truly grown unless you have invested yourself in others.

Normally, a child's growth requires healthy parenting. There are children who grow well even though their parents do not care for them, but these are exceptions. Healthy parental care requires a willingness to sacrifice on behalf of children who may not appreciate what their parents suffer. What is needed in today's church life is this kind of sacrificial care (2 Cor. 12:15).

A Pattern in Trusting God and Investing in Others

David no doubt trained his men to use weapons, work as a team, and fight as an army. However, the critical training David provided them was in putting their trust in the Lord and caring for those they were placed with. David became a pattern to them in these things.

If we want to raise up those the Lord has put with us, we must be a pattern for them in experiencing Christ in every situation and in investing ourselves in others. In all things, they should rely upon no one and nothing other than Christ Himself. This kind of healthy training is crucial if we want them to fight for the Lord in a way that brings in His kingdom.

A Field to Labor In

After being trained by David, this small band of men was able to regain Keilah by defeating the army of the Philistines (1 Sam. 23:1–5). This battle made all their training real and practical.

If we do not have a practical field in which to exercise what we have learned, nothing will come of our training. Some may feel that being a VIP in the church life can substitute for having a field to labor in, but that is not the case. We need to have a practical field to labor in which will bring us to Christ. Our field is where our trust in Christ and care for others becomes practical. In this field we should not exist simply as pawns, but rather we should live fulfilled lives as organic members of the body of Christ, developing and growing in function.

My first field of labor in the church life was serving the children. I began as a teacher but eventually became the leader of the children's service, responsible for training others. Every week each teacher had to do some homework, read the Bible, and grow in the spiritual life. They even had to come together to demonstrate how they would teach their lesson, as well as testify how they had been living before the Lord. Due to that process a number of good teachers were raised up. That is a field.

Later, when I was accepted into my first university, I realized that this could be another field of labor. I rented a room near the campus and began to preach the gospel to the students there. Eventually many got saved.

I first came to the United States in 1963. I worked with one couple, and by the Lord's mercy, from there the work developed into dozens of churches with thousands of Christians in the Great Lakes area, opening for me a large field to labor in.

We should not be satisfied with just living as good churchgoers who obey church leaders and give weekly tithes. Nor should we merely be involved in carrying out activities. Activities will help us develop a skill, but they may not teach us to trust the Lord or care for others. If we are not actively involved in a field of labor, we will simply maintain a good church life, thinking everything is marvelous, when so much more is possible. Therefore, we all should seek a field of labor in our local church to help us know Christ and invest in others.

I am very happy when I hear that a young person has found a field. Young people should fight for this. If they begin to serve the high schoolers, they should not be there merely for fun. They should be able to say it is their commitment from the Lord and should be burdened for it. They should say, "Give me three years, and see what happens. I will raise up ten others to serve with me who share my commitment. Together, we will double the number of high schoolers who love the Lord." This is what it means to have a field of labor.

As you labor in your field, practice to have fresh experiences of Christ. Also, it is better not to labor by yourself, but together with a few others. Invest yourself in others and allow others to invest themselves in you. None of us should be isolated, selfish, or lonely as we labor in our field. We should invest ourselves in one another as we serve together in the church life.

Our Prayer

David worked with whoever the Lord brought to him—the distressed, the debtors, and the discontented. Who but David was willing to work with people like this? He raised them up, forming them into a fighting force to establish his kingdom. Isn't this encouraging? Everyone should pray, "Lord, I am full of problems and don't have much, but I give myself to You to become one of Your mighty men for the sake of Your kingdom, that Your purpose may be accomplished on earth."

7

Overcoming to Bring in the Kingdom

Israel occupied a very small strip of land, and within that small strip, David and his men initially occupied only the cave of Adullam. Starting from this cave, the Lord developed what would become David's kingdom. As David and his army advanced from the cave of Adullam and began moving about Israel and its surroundings, much of their movement was in response to Saul's persecution. During this time, the Lord trained David not to fear but to trust Him unconditionally. David matured to the point that he no longer feared Saul or any other threat. He realized that he was in the Lord's hands and should rest in Him and enjoy His salvation.

Fleeing to the Wilderness

After rescuing Keilah and then fleeing from it, David escaped to the wilderness of Ziph (1 Sam. 23:13–14). Ziph means "flowing" (Strong); in other words, not settled but always on the move. While David was there, Saul sought him every day. Remember, Saul was caught by religion. Those caught by religion persecute others more tirelessly than anyone else on earth. Businessmen realize that competition is a good thing, and politicians use each other to obtain their objectives. Religious zealots, however, try to purge those they view as a threat.

Strangely, though Saul in his zeal could not find David, somehow Jonathan could (1 Sam. 23:15–16). David had hidden himself in the woods, and Jonathan came to him. Eventually the men of Ziph told Saul that David was hiding among them (v. 19). By the time Saul prepared to come to Ziph, David had already moved to the wilderness of Maon. Though he pursued David and nearly trapped him in Maon, Saul heard that the Philistines were attacking Israel and had to leave (vv. 25–28).

Dwelling in En Gedi

David and his men went up from Maon and dwelt in strongholds at En Gedi (1 Sam. 23:1). The name En Gedi means *the fountain of the kid* (Strong). The young of sheep may also be implied.

The psalms David wrote during this period indicate how much he appreciated the Lord as his Savior and recognized his own unworthiness (e.g., Psa. 31). To David, the Lord was like a pure lamb, whereas he himself was an ugly goat. David's psalms from this period reveal that he depended on the Lord for his daily salvation (e.g., Psa. 17:7; 54:1; 57:1). This Lord could not be defeated. David's enemy was powerful, but there was no reason to be afraid, for he had such a Savior.

When we first came to the Lord, we experienced Him as the Lamb of God without spot or blemish (John 1:29; 1 Pet. 1:19). In the light of the Lord's purity and love toward us, we realized how worthless and terrible we were. As we confessed our sins that day, we prostrated ourselves before the Lord in our shame and sense of utter worthlessness. Eventually, we learned to trust not in ourselves but in our resurrected Lord who is able to uphold us, save us, and bring us through. This was David's experience at En Gedi. He learned that he could trust in the Lord.

Encountering Saul in the Cave

After we realize the Lord is with us, we will begin to view our persecutors differently. We will no longer fear them as before.

Saul returned to his search for David at En Gedi after fighting the Philistines. He entered alone into a cave to attend to his needs, not knowing that David and his men were hiding there. As David looked upon him, Saul did not look so mighty. David had been running from Saul, fearing him as a mighty king. Now, however, Saul looked weak and vulnerable. While Saul was in this condition, David secretly cut off a corner of his robe (1 Sam. 24:1–4).

The phrase, "corner of his robe," can also be translated "wing of his robe." When David told Saul what he had done, it seems he was saying, "Look, Saul. I have clipped your wing. You can no longer fly over me as you did before. You have been chasing me all around, but I have now clipped your wing." Saul was no longer in control. Instead, David was able to capture Saul.

As David held up that corner of Saul's robe, he could have told him, "Saul, it's over. I'm tired of you bothering me all the time. Now get out of Israel!" Instead, David's heart troubled him, and he said, "The Lord forbid that I should do this thing to my master, the Lord's anointed, to stretch out my hand against him" (1 Sam. 24:5–6).

Most of us have experienced being troubled by the Lord in our conscience in this way. As we prayed for something or did something, we were checked by the Lord. Is He really our Lord? How often we demand things of Him that He hasn't sought for us. Whatever we seek apart from Him will eventually bring us trouble. Whatever we do according to Him becomes a blessing to us, making us happy because He is happy. This is why the Lord allows us to be exposed through such incidents as David's cutting off the corner of Saul's robe.

David's heart troubled him because he had improperly touched the Lord's anointed. Since the Lord had anointed Saul, he was the Lord's responsibility, not David's. If we are to have a church life, we need to learn this. Whenever we criticize our fellow believers or treat them improperly in the eyes of others, our hearts should trouble us immediately. The Lord is their Lord. It is not our place to criticize them (Rom. 14:10). Every believer is in the Lord's heart. He desires to lead every one of them into glory. If we do not see this and treat our fellow believers with grace, our heart should trouble us.

God allowed Saul to come into the cave, and David saw him for what he was. David even cut his "wing." This showed Saul that he could no longer hurt David. Saul was moved when David revealed what he had done. He realized that David, not Jonathan, would have the throne. Saul, however, soon began to hunt David again. His repentance did not last.

The Death of Samuel

Samuel died while David and his men were at the stronghold of En Gedi (1 Sam. 25:1). If David had not gone through what En Gedi represented, he would not have been prepared for Samuel's death. While he was unsettled at Ziph, he still would have felt he needed Samuel. At En Gedi, however, he had come to know the Lord further as the One who is always able to supply him in His resurrection. It seems the Lord was saying, "From now on, David, you shall rely only upon Me."

Nabal's Foolishness

After dwelling in En Gedi, David went to the wilderness of Paran, which was far to the south. Here, David had his men protect the flocks of a man named Nabal, whose name means "fool" (Strong). Under their watchful care, Nabal had not lost any sheep. When David heard that Nabal was shearing his sheep in Carmel, he sent some of his young men to ask him for supplies, reminding him that they had protected his flocks (1 Sam. 25:2–9).

Nabal responded carelessly and insulted David, calling him just another servant who had broken away from his master. Nabal was so foolish that he did not anticipate the consequences this kind of talk would have. When David heard Nabal's response, he set out for Carmel with 400 armed men to slay him (vv. 10–13).

Abigail's Supplication

When Nabal's wife, Abigail, heard how he had spoken to David's men, she quickly realized she must do something to avert David's wrath. She gathered together two hundred loaves of bread, two skins of wine, five sheep already prepared, five measures of roasted grain, a hundred clusters of raisins, and two hundred cakes of figs and brought them to David. She did not tell Nabal anything, which was wise.

What Abigail brought to David may not have been enough to satisfy his entire army, but it was probably all she could do at the moment. When she saw David, she bowed low before him and said, "On me, my lord, on me let this iniquity be!" (1 Sam. 25:24). She was saying her husband's foolish act was her fault, and to punish him would be unjust. We must learn from Abigail and cover others' mistakes in love (1 Pet. 4:8; James 5:20). If possible, deflect punishment away from those less able to bear it.

Abigail confessed that her husband was foolish, saying, "Please, let not my lord regard this scoundrel Nabal. For as his name is, so is he" (1 Sam. 25:25). She went on to indicate that things would have been different if David had sent his men to her instead of to her husband. She then said, "Since the Lord has held you back from coming to bloodshed and from avenging yourself with your own hand, now then, let your enemies and those who seek harm for my lord be as Nabal" (v. 26). Her understanding was marvelous. Though David was still intent on killing Nabal, Abigail stated that the Lord had held him back from shedding blood by sending her to him. Then she offered David the food she had brought and said, "The Lord will certainly make for my lord an enduring house, because my lord fights the battles of the Lord....It shall come to pass, when the Lord...has appointed you ruler over Israel, that this will be no grief to you, nor offense of heart to my lord, either that you have shed blood without cause, or that my lord has avenged himself" (vv. 28, 30, 31).

Based upon her supplication, David relented and even blessed the Lord for sending her, saying, "Blessed is the Lord God of

Israel, who sent you this day to meet me! And blessed is your advice and blessed are you, because you have kept me this day from coming to bloodshed and from avenging myself with my own hand" (1 Sam. 25:32–33). Her words reminded him who he was and what his stand before the Lord was.

David's response was frank; he did not try to avoid losing face. He was a spiritual man speaking with a spiritual woman. He could have said, "It is too late. We have already taken up our swords." Instead, he told her to go in peace to her house.

Abigail returned home to Nabal, who was feasting like a king and becoming very drunk. The next morning, however, when Abigail told Nabal what had almost happened, "his heart died within him, and he became like a stone" (v. 37). Nabal was probably already overweight, and when he heard about how close he had come to being killed by David, it seems he had a stroke. Ten days later, the Lord struck him, and he died.

David Marries Abigail

Through these events, David met Abigail, Nabal died, and Abigail became free to marry David. Perhaps this was an encouragement to David that the Lord was still with him, even though he was a king without a kingdom. In the tenth chapter of this book, we shall see how the wives of David present us a picture of the church in its process of becoming something of glory. Abigail became the third of David's eight wives in this sequence.

Christian Growth

We expect our Christian growth to proceed ever upward in a straight line, but our experience is full of ups and downs. When you are in a hard place, you should be encouraged, for it means you will soon be up. Likewise, when your Christian life is higher than ever before, be prepared, for you will soon experience a deeper down. Over time, you will discover that the experience of being up and down is normal, for through it all you experience being one with Christ. In David's experience these ups and downs can be clearly observed. When he arrived at the cave of Adullam, that was clearly a down experience. When he recaptured the city of Keilah, that was an up experience. He felt Keilah might be his base, but then Saul appeared, and he was told the people of the town would betray him. That was definitely a down experience. David's experience of growth was in this way, and our experience of growth is in this way too.

David's initial move to Ziph, En Gedi, and then Paran was actually three steps down. Outwardly, everything had been cut off. He had little security or comfort. However, inwardly he was learning to trust the Lord for his salvation. Once he had learned this lesson, the Lord brought him to Ziph once again (1 Sam. 26:1–2). The first time David entered Ziph, he was a fugitive. Now he was different. He had confidence in the Lord. I hope all of us would experience Christian growth in such a way.

David Sparing Saul a Second Time

Saul began again to pursue David. He and his three thousand men set up camp in Ziph. David came right into Saul's camp at night with Abishai, one of his men. They found that the Lord had caused a deep sleep to fall upon Saul and those around him (1 Sam. 26:5–7, 12). Abishai said to David, "God has delivered your enemy into your hand this day. Now therefore, please, let me strike him at once with the spear, right to the earth" (v. 8).

God placed the opportunity to kill Saul into David's hand. Many in this situation would have been sorely tempted to strike Saul down just to put an end to the whole tiresome situation. Saul's continual chasing of David from place to place had been one long unremitting headache. Anyone else might have felt, "Whether it's right or wrong, I will kill him and brave the consequences. Anything has to be better than the kind of life I have been leading because of him!" However, that was not David's response.

David answered Abishai, "Do not destroy him; for who can stretch out his hand against the Lord's anointed, and be guiltless?" (v. 9). David's realization was that since God had anointed Saul as king, Saul was God's responsibility. I hope no one would ever say, "Our church leaders are no good," for on the entire globe no one is good. David acknowledged God's selection in anointing Saul as the king and recognized Saul as the one appointed by God to lead all of Israel ahead of him. We all must realize that God is over all such selections.

Instead of killing Saul, David took Saul's spear and jug of water. Once David had put a great distance between himself and Saul's camp, he called out to Abner, the commander of Saul's army, saying, "Why...have you not guarded your lord the king? ...You deserve to die, because you have not guarded your master, the Lord's anointed. And now see where the king's spear is, and the jug of water that was by his head" (vv. 15–16). David rebuked Abner instead of Saul. He could have laughed at Saul and told him to give up, for the Lord was not with him. By removing Saul's spear and jug of water, David touched Saul's supply and protection. David could have said, "Look, Saul. You can neither fight nor even live. Everything is in my hand. Now go home!" Instead he rebuked Abner for not protecting his master, the anointed king.

Saul Repenting Again

David told Saul that he was driving him from the land of the Lord's inheritance to dwell in the lands of false gods. Yet he didn't blame Saul directly. He said simply, "If the Lord has stirred you up against me, let Him accept an offering. But if it is the children of men, may they be cursed before the Lord" (1 Sam. 26:19). Once again, Saul was very moved by David's actions. Twice he had Saul at his mercy, and twice he let Saul go.

Saul said, "May you be blessed, my son David! You shall both do great things and also still prevail" (v. 25).

Was it finally over? It was not. Saul was caught up in something he no longer could control. Church history demonstrates how impossible it is for those caught with ideology and religion to stop until they have carried out their intention. For instance, in the history of the Plymouth Brethren in England, none were more faithful to John Darby than William Kelly, yet the followers of Darby eventually drove even Kelly out. When religion becomes ideology and ideology replaces Christ, people will do everything in their power to preserve that ideology. Once someone is caught in an ideology, Christ no longer seems to count.

Returning to Gath as a Different Person

David recognized it would be impossible to convince Saul that he was not a threat. Realizing that Saul would one day kill him if he remained in Israel (1 Sam. 27:1), he escaped to the land of the Philistines again. This time, however, he went with his army of six hundred. Again he went to Achish, king of Gath, and dwelt among the Philistines for a year and four months. The rest of his men also dwelt in homes there.

The first time David had gone to Gath, he felt he had to pretend to be mad so he could escape, for someone had told Achish who he was. After he escaped from Gath, he dwelt in the cave of Adullam, where he found that the Lord was his strength. It was there he wrote Psalm 34, which contains the words, "Taste and see that the Lord is good" (v. 8). After this he passed through the experiences of Keilah, Ziph, En Gedi, Paran, and to Ziph once more. Now he came to King Achish as a different David—instead of feigning madness, he comes as commander of an army of six hundred.

Eventually David asked Achish to grant him a place to live outside the king's city, and Achish gave him Ziklag (v. 6). David was still technically a fugitive, but he was now acting as a king. Do you think Achish would have given just anyone a city? He realized David's men were a strong force, so he agreed to give David Ziklag. David had been cast out by religion, but those among the Gentiles respected him.

When David came to Gath the first time, he pretended to be mad for his own survival. When we are young Christians, we also may feel the social pressure at work to go to parties to be accepted. After a number of years of following the Lord and growing as Christians, however, we will no longer feel we have to behave in a way to please people. We are like David in his return to Gath. In the beginning, the world took advantage of us. Now, the world is under us. After passing through some experiences of knowing and trusting the Lord, we are no longer the same. Instead of becoming anxious or pressured in our situation, we reign as kings.

A Personal Testimony

When I began working at Case Western Reserve University library, I was given the title of instructor, although I did not teach. The second year, I was promoted to assistant professor, and the third year I was promoted to associate professor. When my supervisor left to become a director of Ball State University's library, he said he would create a position there for me. By the time he called to offer me the newly created position, I told him I had to turn it down, for the Lord had called me to serve Him full time. He asked whether I would have come if he had called two weeks earlier. I answered that I didn't know, for I would have had to pray about it. Before, I was under my employers, for I was their servant, but now that I am serving the Lord, I am over them, for I am a servant of Christ.

After all of David's experiences of retreating and escaping, he eventually returned to the place where he had first sought refuge outside of Israel. This time, however, the outcome was very different. He asked for a city and received Ziklag, which remained a part of Judah from then on. Shouldn't we be so bold? We should tell the Lord, "I do not want to live a common life.

I would like my Christian life to be so adventurous. As I serve You, I know there will be a lot of downs, but also a lot of ups. I will be persecuted, but I will also have much encouragement. As I go through these things, I will become different, even a reigning king."

8

Gaining the Kingdom and Jerusalem

God brought David through many learning experiences. David had been a shepherd, he had been anointed, and he had proven himself by defeating Goliath and "tens of thousands" of the enemy. He had the people's approval. Though he seemed fit to be king in men's eyes, God knew he needed to pass through even more experiences as a fugitive in the wilderness and even in Philistia. This brought David to the point he was ready to be king.

Becoming king, however, did not make things easier for David. He reigned for forty years, first in Hebron for seven and a half years, and then in Jerusalem for thirty-three years (2 Sam. 5:5). During these forty years, he was still maturing. He had achieved a certain stature as king, but as he ruled, he continued to mature.

In this life, we should never consider that we have arrived at the fullness of God's desire for us. Even when we seem to be mature, we still need to mature further (Phil. 3:12–14). When we grow to a point that we have a ministry, the carrying out of that ministry causes us to grow more. When Paul was sent out from Antioch (Acts 13:1–3), he was already relatively mature, but as he journeyed and labored to raise up churches and believers, he matured further. We should consider David's kingship not primarily as a time of having arrived but as a time during which he continued to mature.

Going Up to Hebron

Saul and three of his sons, including Jonathan, died during a battle with the Philistines (1 Sam. 31:1–6). David did not immediately assume the kingship but rather was very much before the Lord. He didn't ask the Lord to clear the way for him to become king over Israel. He only asked Him whether he should go up to any of the cities of Judah. The Lord told him, "Go up" (2 Sam. 2:1). Then David asked to which city, and the Lord told him Hebron.

Hebron means *society* or *friendship* (Hitchcock), implying fellowship. The Lord intended that as David ruled, he would never leave the Lord's presence. By sending David to Hebron, the Lord seemed to be saying, "I have been with you, and you have sought My face. You are the king now, and your kingship shall begin with an even more intimate fellowship between us."

Though David had a strong army of six hundred men, he still asked the Lord, "Shall I go?" It seemed everything was clear outwardly, but he still wanted a word from the Lord to begin his rule. He then had the further confirmation from the response of the people: the men of Judah made him their king (2 Sam. 2:4).

David Blesses the Men of Jabesh Gilead

The first thing David did as king was to bless the men of Jabesh Gilead who had bravely retrieved Saul's body and the bodies of his sons (1 Sam. 31:11–13; 2 Sam. 2:4–7). Jabesh Gilead was the city Saul had saved from the Ammonites when he first became king. These men were better toward Saul than those of Keilah were toward David. When Saul died, the men of that city retrieved his body and buried it in their city. David blessed them for this. It seems the Lord did not utterly give Saul up. His burial at Jabesh Gilead shows him resting upon his victory there, and David the king, as a type of Christ, recognized that.

Living with the Lord's Coming in View

We will all stand before the Lord one day. What we do today is our preparation for that day. We will each be rewarded according to what we accomplished in this life. I know a servant of the Lord who spoke a word of truth at a Christian conference and afterward was severely criticized and even asked to step down. I feel the Lord will reward him for the faithful stand he took in speaking the truth. We may not feel that we have accomplished much, but the Lord may use what we have done beyond our expectation. Perhaps in one instance you spoke just a few minutes, but because of what you spoke, many might be saved throughout the globe. The Lord's work is grand. Who will be rewarded on that day? It may not be those who did a large work in the Lord's name, but rather those who were faithful to the small commitment given them by the Lord (Matt. 7:22; 25:21). We should be more concerned about winning the Lord's smile on that day than about the turbulence that may result from our actions today. Will the Lord say, "I never knew you; depart from Me" (Matt. 7:23)? This is a serious matter. I would rather have the Lord defend me than have to defend myself before Him. We should simply follow the Lord and have the peace that He will answer for us.

Saul became consumed with jealousy, but this is not how he began in the Lord. Though David suffered much because of Saul, he still blessed the men of Jabesh Gilead for what they did to honor Saul in death. David recognized that Saul would still have something before God because of his faithfulness to what was committed to him while his heart was still right.

May none of us simply live a Christian life or do a Christian work. We should not simply be zealous for something. We must have the Lord's coming in view. What have we done that will stand at the judgment seat? Watchman Nee wrote a hymn with this thought. Daily, he said, he sought to live his life in view of the judgment seat of Christ, that his work might be able to pass through the fire on that day. Paul told us that "the fire will test each one's work, of what sort it is" (1 Cor. 3:13).

Joab and Abner's Competition

After the death of Saul and his three sons in battle, Abner proclaimed Saul's only remaining son, Ishbosheth, king over all Israel (2 Sam. 2:8–10). Only Judah followed David. One day the commanders of the two kings met on opposite sides of a pool in the town of Gibeon (2 Sam. 2:13). Abner, the commander of Ishbosheth's troops, said to Joab, David's commander, "Let the young men now arise and compete" (v. 14). Joab and Abner may have been friends at one time and were boasting to each other about their armies.

"So they arose and went over by number, twelve from Benjamin, followers of Ishbosheth the son of Saul, and twelve from the servants of David. And each one grasped his opponent by the head and thrust his sword in his opponent's side" (2 Sam. 2:15–16). What seems to have begun as a competition grew into a fierce battle between the two sides (v. 17). Abner's men eventually got the worst of it. Perhaps David's men had simply received better training and knew how to work as a team.

This kind of competition still occurs among Christians today. People tend to take sides and form parties. We all have to declare, "We are children of God! We only belong to Christ!" We should have nothing to do with competing parties. I hope none would say that they follow me, for I am not worthy of being followed. I hope everyone would follow Christ! No matter how good the person, the teaching, or the method is, we have to say, "I am for Christ!" Otherwise, we will witness times of needless tragedy.

Abner and his troops had to flee. Though Abner must have been a mighty warrior, he could not outrun Asahel, Joab's brother, who was determined to overtake him. Abner told Asahel to stop chasing him and kill one of his young men instead (v. 21). This reveals that Abner had little concern for those in his care. I hope none of us are like this. Abner used others as pawns to achieve success and make himself look good. Asahel was foolish to pursue Abner in the first place. Perhaps he was caught up with the zeal of killing Abner as the top trophy.

Abner again said to Asahel, "Turn aside from following me.

Why should I strike you to the ground? How then could I face your brother Joab" (v. 22). These two commanders seem to have been good friends and both willingly sacrificed those under their command. They shook hands, and those under them died. We should never treat those under our care as capital. We should never consider those we serve as our strength. They belong to God, not to us.

Asahel was no match for Abner, who killed him with the back end of his spear. Most that died that day, however, were of Abner's army. Three hundred sixty of his men died, while only twenty of Joab's men were killed, including Asahel. Joab afterward killed Abner and was marked by David because of it (2 Sam. 3:27–28, 39).

The Fruit of the Self-life

Abner could not accept David as God's anointed king, and this was a source of much trouble. By making Ishbosheth king, Abner was able to maintain his military leadership. He simply went with what fit his self-interest, which led to the incident at the pool of Gibeon. Three hundred sixty lives were sacrificed to the self-life of their leader. When believers begin to fight, it is those under their care who suffer. We who are the Lord's should never get involved in such ugly things.

If you do not know how to love the Lord Jesus as your Savior and how to appreciate the church He has placed you in, you will never grow properly. Instead, you may love the world and become a Christian worker who does not care about others. I hope all who read this will only care for Christ!

Once I was with some churches that were going through a great trial. I was asked if I thought these churches would begin to separate from one another. I found it difficult to identify with the thought behind the question, for the biblical view is that local churches are not connected organizationally, so they cannot be divided in that sense. If we surrender to organization, we shall live for an institution rather than for Christ and

His church. Anything that goes beyond Christ and the local churches will result in casualties, for people will fight over Christian work and orthodoxy.

Reigning in Jerusalem

After seven years of ruling over Judah in Hebron, the way was opened for David to be finally crowned king of all Israel (2 Sam. 5:1–3). The first thing he did was to capture the city of Jerusalem from the Jebusites (5:6–7). Zion is the name given to the heights of Jerusalem. It is also called the city of David, and David's palace was built there. Before David, the kings and judges ruled from their home towns. Even Samuel did this when he ruled from Ramah. David, however, gained a city named "Foundation of Peace" (Davis, p. 385). This city became the center of God's work. Even we in the New Testament age await the New Jerusalem (Rev. 21:2). The fact that David saw the value of Jerusalem testifies to how much David was a man after God's heart.

God's Confirmation

When Hiram, unasked, sent all the materials and craftsmen to build David a palace, David perceived that the Lord had indeed set him to be king (2 Sam. 5:11–12). David was not presumptuous. It may seem obvious to us that God had indeed chosen David to be king after he was set as king over Judah and then over all Israel. David, however, was not like this; he always sought the Lord's speaking and presence. Therefore, he needed confirmation that what had happened was of the Lord and not merely of man, and Hiram's act provided this.

David's Failures

After David moved to Jerusalem, he took more wives and

concubines (2 Sam. 5:13). He had three wives already—Michal, Ahinoam, and Abigail. Eventually he had eight wives. In Deuteronomy 17:14–17, Moses wrote specifically that the kings who would rule Israel should not multiply wives to themselves, lest their hearts be turned away from the Lord. In this matter, David failed.

David and his men also carried away the idols the Philistines left behind while fleeing from his army (2 Sam. 5:21). Perhaps David's soldiers thought of them as souvenirs or trophies and put them in their own homes. Besides failing by having many wives and concubines, David failed by not taking a strong stand regarding idols. This seems to have been an old problem with David. Much earlier, when David was running from Saul, his wife had used a household image to trick those who sought to kill him (1 Sam. 19:13).

God Overlooks David's Failure

We might think that the Lord should have judged David for these two evils, but the Lord instead seemed quite happy with David. In fact, when David inquired about attacking the Philistines, the Lord proposed that David and He fight them together (2 Sam. 5:23–25). The Lord said, "When you hear the sound of marching in the tops of the mulberry trees, then you shall advance quickly. For then the Lord will go out before you to strike the camp of the Philistines" (v. 24). Together, David and the Lord defeated the Philistines.

We might think David should have feared that God was leading him into a trap, since he had done things condemned by God. This is sometimes our feeling. There are times when the Lord asks us to do something for Him after we have just been defeated. We may feel to say, "Lord, let's do it tomorrow, not today. I am afraid if I do it now, it will fail because You are punishing me." But God works with unworthy men. In spite of his flaws, David was a man after God's heart. Therefore, God worked with him.

Attempting to Bring up the Ark

After David had captured Jerusalem, he sought to bring the ark of God into it. The ark had been in the house of Abinadab ever since the Philistines returned it (1 Sam. 6:1; 7:1). David realized that the kingship and priesthood needed to work together, so the ark had to be brought up so that the people would have a healthy leadership.

David had a cart built for the ark and gathered thirty thousand chosen men to bring the ark into Jerusalem with great honor. It must have been a beautiful wagon. The ark was only to be carried by the Levites (Num. 4:15; 1 Chron. 15:2). That may have seemed too simple to David. However, what God has ordained, God has ordained, and we should not seek to improve it.

As the ark neared Jerusalem, the ox that pulled the cart stumbled. Uzzah took hold of the ark to steady it. For this, God struck down Uzzah, and he died (2 Sam. 6:6–7). This caused David to fear what might happen if he brought the ark into Jerusalem. He stopped the procession and had the ark put in the home of Obed-Edom. The ark stayed in Obed-Edom's home for three months, during which time he and his family were blessed by the Lord (v. 11). Perhaps his business dealings suddenly yielded him a great fortune!

David's Dance in a Linen Ephod

When David heard that Obed-Edom's family was blessed, he was encouraged to bring the ark into Jerusalem. This time, however, the ark was not placed on a cart but was carried.

David, clothed in a linen ephod like the priests, accompanied the ark. It was as if he were saying, "I the king would like to be a priest too. Might I share in this privilege of accompanying the ark?" David stripped off his kingly garments and exchanged them for a priestly one. This was how he served the Lord that day.

Every six paces from Obed-Edom's house to Jerusalem, David sacrificed oxen and fatlings. David danced before the Lord with all his might. How good it would be if we all could be so free before the Lord! When we speak for the Lord, it should not be with fear but boldly with all our might. If that were the case, how prevailing we would be! The whole picture here is a joyful one of David, the Lord, and the Israelites enjoying a wonderful time together.

Michal Despising David's Joy

Michal, David's first wife and the daughter of Saul, looked out of her window and wondered, "Who is that crazy person down there dancing?" Perhaps someone told her, "That's your husband, David." Michal mocked David and said to him, "How glorious was the king of Israel today, uncovering himself today in the eyes of the maids of his servants, as one of the base fellows shamelessly uncovers himself!" (2 Sam. 6:20). I think she meant that he had gone about without his kingly garments on. To her, when he walked about, he should have been recognizable as the king, not just one of the many priests.

David's answer was very good: "It was before the Lord, who chose me...to appoint me ruler over the people of the Lord, over Israel. Therefore I will play music before the Lord" (v. 21). How David must have felt! Here he was, king over the most wonderful people on the earth, with God as his King. Therefore, he danced before the Lord, leaping and whirling. What's more, he said, "I will be even more undignified than this, and will be humble in my own sight" (v. 22). David had such a deep realization that everything in his life had been according to God's mercy. Because of this, he did not despise himself but rather respected what God had done in him. Michal, on the other hand, despised David's joy in the Lord and therefore "had no children to the day of her death" (v. 23).

I hope we all might declare, "Lord, I want to be like David and dance before you with all my strength, to satisfy Your heart."

9

God's House— Its Materials, Builder, and Site

David became king when he was thirty and ruled for forty years. For the first seven years, he was king only over Judah, ruling from Hebron. Soon after he became king over all Israel, he captured the city of Jebus, renamed it Jerusalem, and ruled from there. That was a great matter, for even in eternity God rules from a city named Jerusalem. Eventually David moved the ark of the Lord to Jerusalem and placed it in a tabernacle. What was called the city of David, the city of the king, now became God's city.

Once David had settled into his house and the Lord had given Israel rest from their enemies, David said to Nathan the prophet, "See now, I dwell in a house of cedar, but the ark of God dwells inside tent curtains" (2 Sam. 7:2). In saying this, David implied his desire to build God a house. God had never given David a hint that He desired such a thing. It came out of David's heart. As he was dwelling in his house of cedar, he felt it was not fitting that God would dwell in tent curtains—He should have the best. I hope all believers could have this feeling that God deserves the best.

God's Response of Appreciation

Because David expressed this desire, God sent Nathan to him with a word (2 Sam. 7:4–17). He said to David, "Would you build a house for Me to dwell in?" (v. 5). It seems God was appreciative of David's desire, but did God actually need such a physical house?

In the New Testament, Stephen says, "The Most High does not dwell in temples made with hands, as the prophet says: 'Heaven is My throne, and earth is My footstool. What house will you build for Me? says the Lord, or what is the place of My rest?'" (Acts 7:48–49). God was too big for any temple David could build for Him. However, He appreciated David's desire to provide Him a home among His people in Jerusalem. Whether or not David built God such a place, He would be with His people. Though God didn't need a temple, He still appreciated that David was ready to act out of his love for Him. This is like a young girl telling her father, "Daddy, I'm going to buy you an ice cream cone!" Her father appreciates that she is considering his happiness, even though her offer is unnecessary. We can never overdo loving the Lord. He is happy when we give ourselves to please Him, even though what we do for Him may be unnecessary.

God told David, "I will set up your seed after you...and I will establish his kingdom. He shall build a house for My name, and I will establish the throne of his kingdom forever. I will be his Father, and he shall be My son....And your house and your kingdom shall be established forever before you. Your throne shall be established forever" (2 Sam. 7:12–14, 16). To David, this sounded almost too wonderful to be true.

A Son to Build God's House

God's response to David was tempered. He said, "You have shed much blood and have made great wars; you shall not build a house for My name, because you have shed much blood on the earth in My sight. Behold, a son shall be born to you, who shall be a man of rest; and I will give him rest from all his enemies all around. His name shall be Solomon, for I will give peace and quietness to Israel in his days. He shall build a house for My name, and he shall be My son, and I will be his Father; and I will establish the throne of his kingdom over Israel forever" (1 Chron. 22:8–10).

In these verses, Solomon typifies Christ, "the Son of David" (Matt. 1:1), who truly knows God as His Father and whose throne is "forever and ever" (Heb. 1:8). David had a double blessing from God. On earth, he had Solomon as a son, who would rule Israel and build the temple. From the heavens, Christ would come as "the seed of David" (Rom. 1:3) when He became a man, and would establish a heavenly kingdom (John 18:36). Therefore, David is related to both an earthly kingdom and a heavenly one.

Gathering Materials for God's House

David gathered material for the temple his son would build. He had already gathered much from the people he defeated in battle, and he dedicated this toward the building of God's house. He collected timber and stones, brass and iron, one million talents of silver, and one hundred thousand talents of gold (1 Chron. 22:14). During all his warfare and afflictions, David managed to gather a tremendous store of materials. Perhaps others thought he was storing up these materials for himself when, in fact, they were for the Lord's house.

I hope all who seek to serve the Lord would gather materials for the Lord's building as David did in all his troubles and afflictions. As we carry out our warfare before the Lord, we should also accumulate the spiritual materials typified by iron, brass, silver, and gold. Outwardly we may experience trouble and affliction, but inwardly we should be gathering precious materials for God's building (1 Cor. 3:12).

Iron, Brass, Silver, and Gold

Iron and brass signify God's ruling and judgment. In Revelation, the Lord rules with a rod of iron and stands on feet of brass (19:15; 1:15). As He rules and judges us, iron and brass are produced in us for God's building. Under God's government, we are being judged, disciplined, and regulated. One day the deposit of iron and brass in us will qualify us to reign with Christ for one thousand years (Rev. 20:6).

The more we experience the ruling of God (iron) and the judgment of God (brass), the more we realize our need of salvation through Christ's redemption (silver) and God's divine nature (gold). We begin to realize that we need salvation in our thoughts, in our decisions, in our emotions, and in our actions—including our way of eating and manner of dress. Eventually, the Lord's salvation must reach every area of our lives.

David's Failures

Those in a position of authority become vulnerable in certain matters. David had this problem after becoming king. First, he acted as though he were above the law; second, he succumbed to favoritism; third, he became proud in his success.

Acting as if Above the Law—
David and Bathsheba

After David had been king for some time, he began to act as though he were above the law. This got him into serious trouble, as seen in 2 Samuel 11–12. One day as he walked on the roof of his house in Jerusalem, he looked down and saw Bathsheba bathing. Some might wonder whether Bathsheba had set this up, but even if this were true, David was the one who took advantage of it and disobeyed God's law. He sent for her and committed adultery with her. When he discovered that she was with child, he tried to arrange for her husband to sleep with her and thus cover up his deed.

Bathsheba's husband was Uriah, one of David's mighty warriors (1 Chron. 11:26, 41). Because he was such a loyal soldier, he refused to spend time with his wife while his fellow soldiers were suffering on the field of battle, so David's cover-up did not work. David then plotted to have Uriah killed by ordering Joab to send him to the battlefront and then withdraw the troops around him until he was exposed and killed. It is hard to believe David could do anything as terrible as this, but he did. Uriah was thus killed, and David took Bathsheba for his own wife. She bore him the son she had conceived with him.

God's Response through Nathan

After all this had taken place, God sent Nathan to David to touch his conscience by means of a parable. Nathan told David of two men—one rich and one poor. The poor man had nothing but a little lamb which he treasured dearly. The rich man had many flocks and herds. One night when a visitor came, the rich man didn't want to kill one of his own lambs, so he stole the poor man's lamb and prepared it for his guest. When David heard this, he became very angry and declared, "As the Lord lives, the man who has done this shall surely die!" (2 Sam. 12:5). Nathan then said the memorable words, "You are the man" (v. 7). He told him the sword would never depart from his house, and that the child born to Bathsheba through his adultery would die. Though David confessed his sin, the child did die, and the sword has never fully departed from David's house in Israel, even to this day.

By condemning the rich man in the parable, David condemned his own actions. He had killed his own follower to take his wife, when he already had a house full of wives and concubines. By his own admission, David deserved to die for what he had done. Why had he not felt this way before? As king, he unconsciously felt he was not bound by the same limitations others were. He thought he was above the law. This was David's first failure as king—not restricting himself due to a feeling of status.

We must be careful, for if we find ourselves thinking we have gained some status among the Lord's children, we also may feel we can say and do what others cannot. Others must read the Bible, but not us. Others must have a time to pray, but we no longer have such a need. Others must rise up to touch the Lord in the morning, but this no longer applies to us who are more senior. This is wrong. Regardless how spiritual we become, we should never despise the commandment of the Lord (2 Sam. 12:9). The more mature we are, the more we should value the practices that lead to a healthy Christian life and church life. We should never feel we are above such things.

David's Repentance—Psalm 51

David's repentance is found in Psalm 51. It begins, "Have mercy upon me, O God, according to Your lovingkindness; according to the multitude of Your tender mercies, blot out my transgressions" (v. 1). David realized how much he needed the Lord's mercy in abundance. In verse 5, he says he was a sinner from his mother's womb. David expressed his fear as he cried, "Do not cast me away from Your presence, and do not take Your Holy Spirit from me" (v. 11). What he had done was dreadful; he realized it would not suffice simply to offer the Lord some sacrifice. In spite of his unworthiness, David requested, "Do good in Your good pleasure to Zion; build the walls of Jerusalem" (v. 18). It seems David was saying, "Though I have failed, don't allow Your testimony to fail. In spite of me, do good to Zion." His desire was still for the fulfillment of God's desire. I feel that by the time he finished writing this psalm, many of his sins had been cleared up.

Succumbing to Favoritism— David and Absalom

The second test for those in leadership is whether or not they will succumb to favoritism. Leaders nearly always exercise some amount of favoritism. When those in authority do not lead impartially according to merit, unrest and competing parties can result. In spite of all this, it is difficult for leaders not to love some more than others.

David loved his son Absalom. The Bible says that from head to toe, Absalom had no blemish and had incredibly thick hair (2 Sam. 14:25–26). One day he killed one of his half-brothers for taking advantage of his sister. Afterward, he fled, and "David mourned for his son every day" and "longed to go to Absalom" (13:37, 39). After three years, Joab found a way to return Absalom to Jerusalem, even though David would not see him (2 Sam. 14). Eventually, however, David did receive him back. Absalom quickly used his restored princely status to work against his father (2 Sam. 15). He sat at the gate and met with the people before they went to David and told them, "Oh, that I were made judge in the land, and everyone who has any suit or cause would come to me; then I would give him justice" (v. 4). Absalom stole the people's hearts away from his father, the king.

Eventually Absalom asked David permission to go to Hebron to fulfill a vow, and David allowed him to go. His real intent, however, was to be crowned king in Hebron, where David had also been crowned as king over Judah. When David heard that the people favored Absalom, he and his family fled Jerusalem. He knew that if Absalom caught them, he would kill them and perhaps begin a slaughter within Jerusalem itself.

What brought this upon David? His favoritism. He should have left Absalom in exile rather than accept Joab's remedy. Joab represents the flesh, with its good plans. Eventually Absalom was cornered by Joab's troops and fled on a mule, but his head got caught in a tree and he was left hanging in midair. This made him an easy target for Joab's spear. When David heard that his son was dead, he mourned greatly over him, saying, "O my son Absalom—my son, my son Absalom—if only I had died in your place!" (2 Sam. 18:33). He could not be comforted. The entire nation became troubled by this. They had stood with David against Absalom, and now he was inconsolably lamenting the one they had succeeded in killing for his sake. Oh, favoritism is a hard thing to get over!

Because David was unable to act on behalf of the kingdom, Joab rebuked him, saying, "You have disgraced all your servants who today have saved your life...in that you love your enemies and hate your friends....I perceive that if Absalom had lived and all of us had died today, then it would have pleased you well" (2 Sam. 19:5–6). That was a good rebuke. Then he instructed David, "Arise, go out and speak comfort to your servants. For I swear by the Lord, if you do not go out, not one will stay with you this night" (v. 7). David was so consumed with grief over Absalom, he forgot his responsibility to his people. Joab's frank word brought him back to reality. He met with the people at the gate and they were encouraged. This entire situation would have been averted if only David had not exercised favoritism toward Absalom.

Becoming Proud in Success— Numbering the People

Leaders can also be stumbled by becoming proud of their accomplishments and trying to gauge their success by taking inventory. Businessmen can do this, but spiritual men should not. David committed a sin by numbering the people to measure his strength. When we do such a thing, we are looking for strength in something other than God. It is too easy to take pride in things other than the Lord Himself.

If someone receives Christ through us, or if the Lord blesses others through us, we should be joyful about it, but not for our own glory. Church growth should be for the Lord's interest, not ours. Too often we become proud after leading someone to Christ; it becomes a boast for us. When my companions and I first served the Lord while in high school, over one hundred were saved through our gospel preaching. I am still tempted to boast in that number, even though that occurred over fifty years ago! This is simply in our blood.

David realized he had sinned in numbering the people. He told the Lord, "I have sinned greatly in what I have done; but now, I pray, O Lord, take away the iniquity of Your servant, for I have done very foolishly" (2 Sam. 14:10). He had forgotten that from the beginning, the Lord told him that He Himself was the real King.

God gave David three options for punishment—seven years of famine, three months fleeing from his enemies, or three days of plague. David simply said, "Please let us fall into the hand of the Lord, for His mercies are great; but do not let me fall into the hand of man" (v. 14). Therefore, God caused a plague among the people that eventually killed seventy thousand. An angel appeared at the threshing floor of Ornan. David hurried to buy that threshing floor, built an altar there, and sacrificed burnt offerings and peace offerings to the Lord. The Lord heeded David's actions and withdrew the plague from the land.

That threshing floor became the location of the temple. Even out of David's defeat, something was gained for the Lord. The Lord works with unworthy men for His testimony. According to our thought, God should not work with someone who fails Him, yet God will always use those who have a heart for Him, regardless how badly they fail Him. Out of David's sin involving Bathsheba and Uriah, Solomon, the builder of the temple, was gained, and out of his sin of numbering the people, the site for the temple was gained.

After all these failures, we still have to appreciate David. His heart toward God allowed God to gain something for His purpose through him, even though his actions should have disqualified him. God was able to use David in spite of his failures because David was a man after God's heart and sought to serve his generation as such a king.

10

David's Wives

In Ephesians, Paul likens the relationship between Christ and the church to that of a husband and wife (5:22–32). Based on this, a number of Bible scholars teach that if a man in the Old Testament typifies Christ, then his wife may be a type of the church. For instance, Adam typifies Christ, therefore Eve typifies the church— just as Eve came from Adam when he was put to sleep, the church was produced when Christ was put to sleep on the cross. Since David typifies Christ as the One who establishes God's kingdom, his eight wives should show us something about the church.

Michal

David's first wife was Michal (1 Sam. 18:27). Her name means "who is perfect?" (Hitchcock) or "rivulet" (Strong), a small brook. Michal signifies something of our initial experience of the church life. We sense we are imperfect and need salvation. We may even feel discouraged about ourselves. Yet when we meet together, we are brought to something pleasant, refreshing, and flowing, like a clear, bubbling brook. Though we feel inadequate and unworthy, we also feel encouraged and renewed.

Ahinoam

David's second wife was Ahinoam (1 Sam. 25:43), which

means "brother of pleasantness" (Easton) or "beauty of the brother" (Hitchcock). As we enjoy the bubbling-brook church life, we begin to appreciate how beautiful our Christian brothers and sisters are. We are drawn to them and desire to spend time with them.

Abigail

David's third wife was Abigail (1 Sam. 25:42), which means "the father's joy" (Hitchcock). The more we appreciate our brothers and sisters in the church life, the more we are brought into the Father's joy.

Before finding David, Abigail had married Nabal, a very evil man whose name means "fool" (Strong). We all come into the church life already married to some "husband" such as a company, career, or school. Regardless how much we give ourselves to these, they do not care a bit about us.

Abigail was known for her wisdom (1 Sam. 25:3). When Nabal insulted David, Abigail saved the situation by acting wisely. Nabal then died, freeing Abigail to become David's wife. Therefore, if we wish to enjoy the Father, we must allow the Lord to liberate us from our old husband so that we might be free to be joined to Him (Rom. 7:2–3). We must pray, "Lord Jesus, for the sake of the church, free me from everything that prevents You from being my Husband!"

Maacah

David's fourth wife was Maacah (2 Sam. 3:3). Her name means "pressed down" or "worn" (Hitchcock). While we are in the church life, sometimes we may feel pressed down or worn. If we are not enjoying Christ afresh, the church life will seem dull and routine. Apart from Christ, the church life is boring, but when Christ is fresh and real to us, it truly is enjoyable. Therefore, when we feel worn down in the church life, we need to come to the One who is always fresh and new!

We should not be discouraged by a period during which we don't seem to be making any progress, for as we trudge wearily on, we are growing, and that growth will bring us into another stage, even that of renewed feasting.

Haggith

David's fifth wife was Haggith (2 Sam. 3:4), whose name means "festive" (Brown) or "rejoicing" (Hitchcock). As we experience the Lord in the down times as well as the up times, we begin to have a new level of appreciation of who the Lord is and what He has done. The church life becomes a place of increased feasting and enjoyment.

Abital

David's sixth wife was Abital (2 Sam. 3:4). Her name means "father of the dew" or "father of the shadow" (Hitchcock). The church life is a very romantic place! Sometimes, we enjoy something so fresh and heavenly, and at other times we are brought into a land of shadows. Could we ever have imagined that while we follow the Lord in the church life, He would bring us into the shadow of death so we could experience the dew of resurrection (Psa. 23:4)? And after experiencing the fresh dew of the morning, we are brought again into shadows. The church life is a most marvelous place.

Eglah

David's seventh wife was Eglah (2 Sam. 3:5), which means "heifer" (Hitchcock). According to 1 Samuel 16:2, Samuel sacrificed a heifer when he anointed David to be king. As we grow in the church life, we experience being anointed more and more by passing through all these experiences. Increasingly, we become a blessing to all the saints with us.

Bathsheba/Bathshua

Bathsheba was David's eighth wife (2 Sam. 11:27). Her name means "daughter of an oath" (Brown) or "daughter of satiety" (Hitchcock), that is, daughter of satisfaction. She was also called Bathshua (1 Chron. 3:5), which means "daughter of wealth" (Brown). We are able to be brought on to maturity because in the church life each of us, as an heir of promise, is a daughter of God's oath (Heb. 6:17). Our ability to serve the Lord is not based on ourselves but on God's ability to fulfill His oath. Sometimes our situation seems precarious, as though we are walking on marbles, yet we are still able to serve. At any moment we could fall were it not for the Lord who is trustworthy.

As we trust in the Lord, we find full satisfaction in Him. Regardless of what we pass through, we are daughters of satisfaction. The Lord is our satisfaction throughout our experience of the church life. Eventually, we become a "daughter of wealth" by enjoying the triune God in the church life. When we consider those around us in the church life, we realize some have become spiritually wealthy. They are rich before the Lord in their experience, service, and ability to render blessings to others in the body of Christ.

11

David's
Mighty Men

The record of David's mighty men provides a very good picture of the various kinds of ministries necessary for the kingdom life to be established in the church today (1 Cor. 12:5). Each of these mighty men accomplished something representing an area of ministry, a "field" in which we may serve. We need such a field if we wish to grow. Without a field, there is no way to be manifested as a "mighty man," for the Bible records very specific things accomplished by the mighty men. Today we need to function in a way that produces a specific blessing in the church. The eleven cases of mighty men specifically mentioned in the Bible portray eleven fields of service. A complete and functional church life needs all eleven fields experienced and applied at various times.

These mighty men were produced in three groups. The first group came to David while he was taking refuge in the cave of Adullam. A second group came to David before he went to Ziklag to help him gain the kingdom. Then, after David was received as king in Hebron, many came to him to help build up the kingdom. Some from each of these groups became mighty men who fought alongside David for the sake of God's earthly kingdom.

Mighty Men for the Kingdom

David's mighty men fought for the sake of their king and the establishment of his kingdom. This is the mark of true mighty men. They were not mighty to establish something for themselves. As we preach the gospel or serve in various fields, our aim should only be Christ and His kingdom.

What is this kingdom? Today, Christ is the reality of this kingdom, expressed practically through His body on the earth as local churches. These churches are the desire of God, so all the mighty men must fight for Christ to become the reality of all the believers in their church. In this way, the universal body of Christ will be expressed in their local church. Any ministry that does not serve the local churches is not a ministry that is according to God's desire. God wants us to gain Christ, and this Christ whom we are gaining desires to be manifested on this earth through local churches.

Therefore, we should not look down on our church. Even if Christ can hardly be seen there, it is still His expression, because He is its content. This is what our "mightiness" is for. The stronger our church, the more prevailing will be the manifestation of Christ. If we serve with the local churches in view, the bride of Christ shall be made ready for the Lord.

Trained to Become Mighty Men

The mighty men became mighty because they gave themselves to David to be trained. In order for us to serve the Lord as one of His mighty men, we also must be trained. Any mightiness we possess for the building up of God's kingdom does not come about by chance. Fight for any opportunity to be effectively trained. How will this take place? As the Lord provides! One way is through formal training. Another is by those more advanced in the Lord raising up those who are younger. I encourage all who graduate from college to devote at least one year to this. After such a year, I believe they will become much more operative in their church. Some might feel led of the Lord to find employment while others might feel to remain unencumbered for His service. In this way, they will become mighty men for the Lord whether they work or serve Him full time.

There is a real difference between dutiful service and effective service. If we do not take the way of training, we may reach old age with little to show for it other than position and seniority. Instead of training those younger than us in the Lord, we may hold onto our position, effectively blocking their advance. Those who have obtained a leadership position rarely give it up easily. Some are unable to give up their position, not because they possess a genuine ministry, but because they feel it is all they have to show for their years of service. To avoid becoming such a blockage, we should give ourselves to the Lord to be trained so we may become effective in our service. May we all be trained to serve effectively in a field of labor for the building up of the Lord's kingdom.

Obtaining Bethlehem's Water for David

One day David cried with longing, "Oh, that someone would give me a drink of the water from the well of Bethlehem..." (2 Sam. 23:15). The way David's men responded to his longing shows us something about the mighty men he trained. Consider what carrying out such a longing required—the roads must have been watched, so their travel would not be easy; Bethlehem was occupied by a troop of Philistines, so they would have to break through the garrison. To provide such a drink hardly seemed reasonable, for water from any other place would have been just as able to quench David's thirst. Since David desired this particular water, however, three of his men embarked on a mission to bring David the water he desired (v. 16).

David expressed this longing during the harvest time (v. 13), a time when everyone is very occupied. It is a time of blessing. How wonderful it is to be occupied in the Lord's work when it is "in season" (2 Tim. 4:2; Gal. 6:9)—the gospel is bearing fruit; people are getting saved; the work is blessed! Then, just as we are preparing to baptize some more people, the Lord says, "Can you stop what you are doing and provide Me with a drink of water?" At that moment do we have the heart to drop everything and simply satisfy the Lord's thirst, letting Him know how much we love Him? Can we serve the Lord as we work for Him? If we desire to be counted among the Lord's mighty men, this is the chief requirement.

When we are feeling dry in a time that is "out of season," we may kneel down often and tell the Lord we love Him, because there is little else to do. But when the Lord blesses the work, and there is so much to be occupied with, can we still tell the Lord, "Lord, we are laboring to quench not only man's thirst, but Yours as well. We love You." We may feel we are only medium-strong mighty men in the Lord's army, but we still bring Him the water He desires.

Understanding the Times

Two hundred chief men of Issachar came to David at Hebron. These men "had understanding of the times, to know what Israel ought to do" (1 Chron. 12:32). This shows us that once a church has been established, there is a need for those with understanding of the times who know what to do.

The church needs those who possess the ability to see the real situation. Some have no thought of the current need of the church but are satisfied just to enjoy the meetings. Others, however, have developed the ability to discern the church's specific need at any given time. For instance, is it time for the church to focus on the gospel? Is it time for a conference on a certain matter? Is it time to focus on the young people? Is it time for some of the young believers to visit another church? Why is it that many eventually end up saying, "We missed it! If only we had done this or that at the time. Now the opportunity is gone." It is because they do not know how to work according to the times. Solomon tells us that everything has a season (Eccl. 3:2). There is a season to sow, a season to grow, and a season to harvest. Where are those who have the ability to discern the times and the seasons?

In the church life, there is a need for some who have the

ability to lead in this way, who know what the church should do. They must develop the ability to discern how the Spirit is working at that particular time and endeavor to cooperate with the Spirit's move. The more who possess this ability, the better. There were two hundred such men with David. For the spread of the kingdom throughout the land, many with such discernment are needed.

Josheb-Basshebeth: Forming the Army

Josheb-Basshebeth proved himself to be a mighty man by killing eight hundred men at one time (2 Sam. 23:8). This ability to slaughter the enemy qualified him to become chief among the captains in David's army. Before the mighty men could fight together as an army, they needed someone like Josheb-Basshebeth who not only knew how to fight himself, but also knew how to form them into an army. We shouldn't just dream about raising up others for the Lord. We must first know how to destroy the enemy ourselves. May there be some among us who are not only able to fight for the Lord, but also able to bring together others as an army to do the same.

Shammah: Defending the Field

Shammah "stationed himself in the middle of the field, defended it, and killed the Philistines" (2 Sam. 23:11–12). This field represents our local church. There is a great need for mighty men who know how to protect their church life from the enemy's onslaught.

The enemy uses many devices (2 Cor. 2:11). When he tries to take over a local church, he may bring in something sinful, something worldly, or an ideology and thus neutralize a church's ability to express the Lord. Some need to know how to prevent the enemy from bringing these things in.

Shammah's name means "astonishment" (Hitchcock). We

should feel astonished when we see worldliness among God's children, or when we see sinfulness creep in. We should say, "What! Sin, do you dare come in and defile us? World, do you think you can simply walk in and contaminate us? Ideology, are you trying to gain a foothold to turn us into a religion?" Each of us should respond, "I will defend what the Lord has gained among us with my life! I will give myself to slaughter any Philistine who dares enter this field!" I hope many young people will tell their parents, "Let's work to defend this field together. Whatever tries to invade—sin, the world, ideology, religion— let's strike it down dead."

Often what the enemy tries to do doesn't look alarming at first. Perhaps it is something that becomes more culturally acceptable over time. Many seemingly innocent things have a long-term effect, opening the door to the attitudes and reasonings of the world. If we hear that one of our fellow believers is being choked by "the cares of this world and the deceitfulness of riches" (Matt. 13:22), our response should not be to sleep. If we hear that someone is getting swallowed up by his career, we should know how to wage warfare so that the enemy is driven back. Such mighty men are sober and watchful over the situation and know when and how to take up the sword.

How we need such mighty men in the church life today! Sin, the world, and religion should not be able to find any place in our church life. The church should be a field for growing only Christ. If every local church had a few warriors guarding it against sin, the world, and religion, how good that would be!

Abishai: Defending the Lord's Kingdom

Abishai was a very powerful warrior for the kingdom (2 Sam. 23:18). On just one occasion he killed three hundred of the enemy. He was not as powerful as Josheb-Basshebeth, who killed eight hundred, but he was still a mighty warrior. The

Bible does not give the nationality of this enemy. Abishai simply fought anyone who rose up against the Lord's kingdom. May the Lord give us such a vigilant heart to defend His interest against any and all who come against it.

Benaiah: Slaying the Sinful and Material World

Benaiah was a mighty man who slew "two lion-like heroes of Moab," "a lion in the midst of a pit on a snowy day," and an Egyptian, "a spectacular man," with the Egyptian's own spear (2 Sam. 23:20–21).

Being lion-like refers to being empowered by Satan himself (1 Pet. 5:8). Furthermore, the source of Moab was incest, a terrible sin (Gen. 19:36–37). The entire world is under the influence of Satan (1 John 5:19), and the element he uses to control people is sin. For instance, although computers themselves are not sinful, they have become a means for many to become involved in sin. No matter how innocent something in the world might seem, it can be used to bring a person into sin. A necklace seems quite innocent, yet if a young woman desires it badly enough, she may lie to get it, telling her parents that she needs money for a textbook. Thus, an innocent item in the world has involved someone in sin.

Benaiah slew a lion in a time of snow, a time of hardship. We too should overcome the influence of Satan so that we might not become involved with sin, even in a time of hardship or temptation.

Benaiah also slew an Egyptian. Egypt represents the material or physical world. I was once offered a luxury car at a very reasonable price. At my age, riding in a small car leaves me achy all over, making it difficult to stand and speak when I arrive at my destination. It takes me a while to recover from such a trip. Thus, I could have justified buying the luxury car. I declined to buy it, however, because it could have caused others to strive after such things. I have to be careful about how my actions affect others. We need to guard our hearts from both the elements of the material world and the sinful world that the church might possess only Christ.

Keeping Battle Formation

Among David's army were many who were recognized as having the ability to keep battle formation (1 Chron. 12:35–36). In time of war, how the forces are arrayed upon a battlefield is crucial, and these forces must be able to quickly rearrange themselves at their leader's command. The best leader and the best fighting men can still lose if they do not know how to arrange themselves. This is often the reason battles have been won or lost throughout history. In the same manner, church leaders today, whether leaders of the whole church or of smaller groups within the church, should consider how to group the members according to their strength, situation, and need.

Expert in All the Weapons of War

An army needs many experts in the art of combat. Those who came to David of Zebulun, Reuben, Gad, and the half-tribe of Manasseh were "expert in war with all weapons of war" (1 Chron. 12:33, 37). We need to become experts in the weapons God has given us today, which include the Bible, hymns, and spiritual books. If we only know one verse in the Bible, we will not be able to bring every person to Christ. Once I invited someone to come preach the gospel among us. A year later I invited him again, and he preached the same message, because that was the only message he knew. On the one hand, to have one message is better than to have none, but to be "expert in war" we need to be familiar with all the available "weapons of war."

Some in a church need to know what hymn or song matches the current need. They should be very familiar with the available hymns and songs. Some need to be familiar enough with the Bible to locate verses to answer questions. Some need to be so familiar with spiritual books that they can point others to helpful ministry regarding such topics as the forgiveness of sin, consecration, and the experience and enjoyment of the Lord. We need to develop a familiarity with all the available instruments of our warfare.

The broader the base of expertise we develop, the more the Lord will be able to use us in the future. This is especially crucial for young people. The church needs those who know how to utilize all the weapons the Lord has provided for our warfare.

Equipping Ourselves

The mighty men from the tribe of Benjamin who came to David at Ziklag while he was still fleeing from Saul were led by Ahiezer (1 Chron. 12:1–3), whose name means "brother of assistance" (Hitchcock). They had the ability to shoot arrows and sling stones with the right or left hand equally well.

Many of us may feel that we do not have the spiritual equivalent of the abilities possessed by David's mighty men. They were so powerful and so able to do whatever was necessary to successfully battle against any enemy. Perhaps we are not yet so able as this, but at least we can memorize John 3:16: "God so loved the world that He gave His only begotten Son...." Once we know this verse, it becomes a slingstone or arrow in our arsenal. Knowing just one verse, however, is not sufficient. We need another, such as Mark 16:16: "He who believes and is baptized will be saved; but he who does not believe will be condemned." As we become more able to quote from the Bible, we will find that we possess an ability to sling stones and shoot arrows. We may not be as mighty as some, but when we arrive at the battle line, we can help others receive the Lord as their Savior, or help young believers to better know their Lord. Every Christian should at least develop in this way. We should not merely wish to be a mighty man or claim to be one; we need this kind of basic training. Everyone should be familiar with enough of the Bible to help someone come to faith in Christ and to love Him more.

Swift as Gazelles upon the Mountains

Eleven Gadites, captains of the army, were expert in handling shields and spears and were "as swift as gazelles on the mountains" (1 Chron. 12:8–9). Mountains represent resurrection. After a defeat, we need to know how to experience resurrection and be restored to stand again to fight for the Lord. When confronting some enemies, these mighty men could fight with shields and spears, and when needed, they could be as swift as gazelles to escape. God is so gracious. Some might feel incapable of doing anything in this warfare, but at least they can develop the ability to run. When sin comes, we should know how to flee (2 Tim. 2:22, 1 Tim. 6:11). When the enemy attacks, we should be able to say, "You can't catch me!" Some are able to kill eight hundred of the enemy, others three hundred, but that may not be us. If we cannot attack, we can still defend...and run real fast! David's mighty men were not all of equal might. We can still be a "mighty man" before the Lord even if we do not feel we are as mighty as someone else.

Attacking as Commandos

The final mention of David's mighty men refers to those who led the troops of Manasseh against the invading raiders (1 Chron. 12:20–21). They were like commandos whose job was to deal with the raiders by going from city to city. They would have had to attack quickly before the enemy could react. This is like those who travel to a city for a three-day gospel campaign, infuse a burning gospel spirit, and then return home.

Some of us should begin to labor as commandos going from place to place to produce something before the enemy can respond. By the time we leave, something will have happened; something will have been produced that wasn't there before we arrived. May the Lord stir us up to become such mighty men, able to join others on such missions.

Once a new church has been raised up through a gospel

campaign, some will need wisdom to see what is necessary and when. Some will also need to be able to group the new believers in the best possible way. Others will need to raise up new leaders. Many should become experts in spiritual combat. There will even be the need of those who know how to defend themselves so they can be preserved to fight in the future. These are the necessary fields of service needed for a complete and functional church life.

These were David's mighty men. They were not mighty for themselves; their might was for God's kingdom. David, the man after God's heart, led them. Like David and those he raised up, may we today not seek our own things but rather what blesses the Lord, until His throne is established on earth. All the mighty men will then rejoice to see the fruit of their labor and rest in it on that day.

Until then, we fight.

Works Cited

Brown, Francis, Samuel R. Driver, Charles A. Briggs, and Wilhelm Gesenius. *A Hebrew and English Lexicon of the Old Testament.* London: Oxford University Press, 1939.

Davis, John D. *Dictionary of the Bible.* Nashville: Royal Publishers, Inc., 1973.

Easton, Matthew G. *Illustrated Bible Dictionary.* Thomas Nelson, 1897.

Hitchcock, Roswell D. *New and Complete Analysis of the Holy Bible.* 1869.

Nee, Watchman. *A Table in the Wilderness.* Wheaton: Tyndale House Publishers, Inc., 1978.

Strong, James. *A Concise Dictionary of the Words in the Hebrew Bible.* Madison, NJ, 1890.

Young, Robert. *Analytical Concordance to the Bible.* Grand Rapids: Wm. B. Eerdmans Publishing Co., 1970.

Online Ministry by Titus Chu

MinistryMessages.org is the online archive for the ministry of Titus Chu. This includes audio messages, articles, and books in PDF format, all of which are available as free downloads.

FellowshipJournal.org is an online magazine that features recent sharing by Titus Chu. It also provides brief, daily excerpts from his ministry, as well as news of upcoming events.

"Daily Words for the Christian Life" is an e-letter sent out every Thursday. It features selections from the writings of Titus Chu. To subscribe, visit FellowshipJournal.org/subscribe.

Books by Titus Chu

The books listed below are available in print, Kindle, or iBook format. To purchase them, go to MinistryMessages.org/order. They are also available via Amazon.com and iTunes.

David: After God's Heart

Elijah & Elisha: Living for God's Testimony

Ruth: Growth unto Maturity

Philippians: That I May Gain Christ

A Sketch of Genesis

Two Manners of Life

www.ingramcontent.com/pod-product-compliance
Lightning Source LLC
Chambersburg PA
CBHW031625040426

42452CB00007B/682